Iron Horse Art Coloring Book
Pen & Ink Railroad Art
By Don Kirk

Published by
SWEETWATER STAGELINES™
An imprint of
THE OLD WEST COMPANY™
5118 Village Trail Drive
San Antonio, Texas 78218

Tradepaper (ISBN13): 978-0-9898004-4-0
Printed and bound in the United States of America

Other Pen & Ink Coloring Books By Don Kirk:
Western Art Coloring Book Vol I
Western Art Coloring Book Vol II
Sundry Art Coloring Book

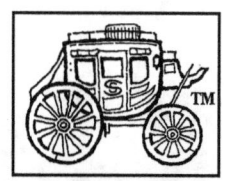

SWEETWATER STAGELINES™
SAN ANTONIO, TEXAS

Iron Horse Art Coloring Book

Pen & Ink

Railroad Art

By Don Kirk

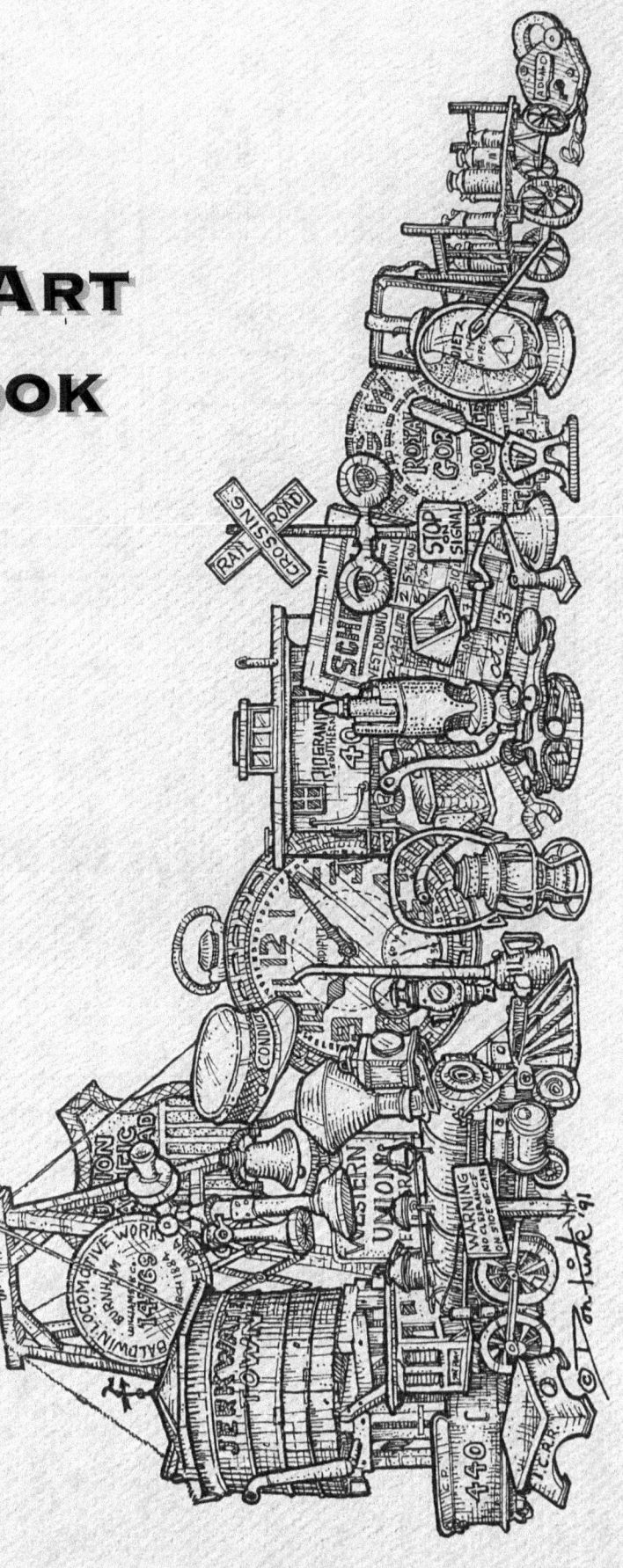

POSTCARD

_____

_____

_____

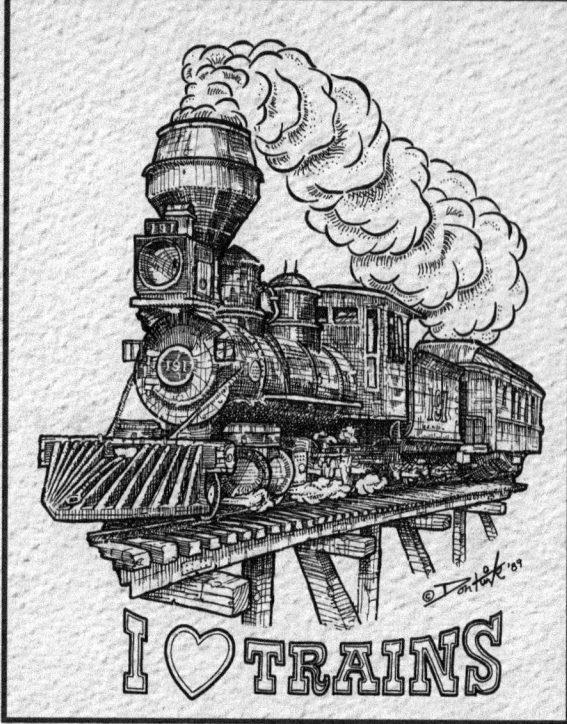

I ♥ TRAINS

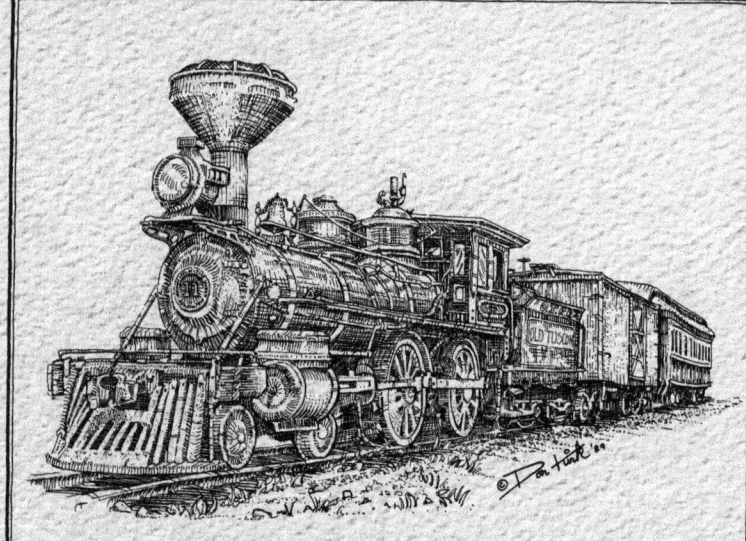

VIRGINIA & TRUCKEE NO. 11 #202P

The Virginia & Truckee No. 11, a 4-4-0 built by Baldwin Locomotive Works in 1872, was purchased by MGM in 1945 where it remained until sold to "Old Tucson", Arizona in 1970. With the photogenic V & T-style "sunflower" stack, it was used in hundreds of westerns and commercials. Originally a woodburner, she was converted to coal in 1886 and then to oil in 1905. Her cylinders are 16X24 inches, boiler pressure: 130 lbs., driver diameter: 57 inches, engine weight: 65,000 lbs and a traction effort calculated to be 11,920 lbs.

THE C. P. HUNTINGTON #204P

The "C. P. Huntington", a tiny 4-2-4 woodburning locomotive with one driving axle, was built by Danforth, Cook and Company in 1863 for the Central Pacific lines. It was only 29 feet long and weighed just 39,000 pounds. A standard gauge engine, she has 11X15 inch cylinders, 54 inch drivers, a boiler pressure of 110 pounds and a traction effort of 3,510 lbs. Completely restored to mint condition, she is on display at the California State Railroad Museum, Sacramento, California.

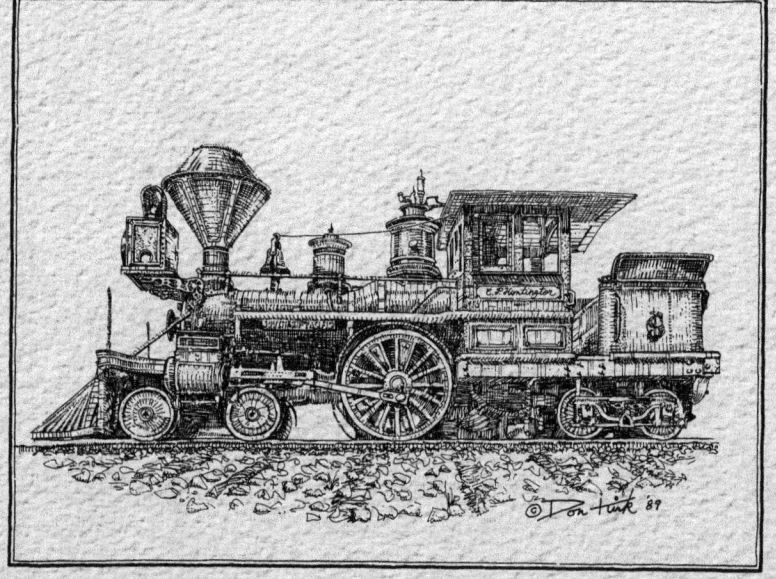

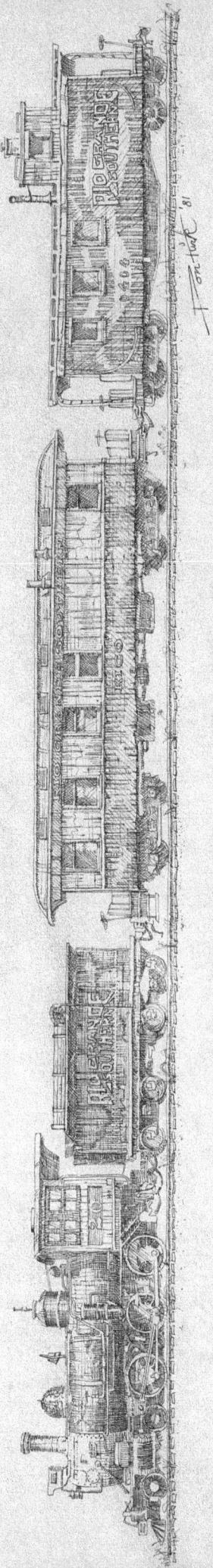

Don Kirk has been traveling the West searching for the spirit of those men and machines that toiled to bring commerce to a wild land. He found rusty hulks of iron, abandoned depots, and trackside relics of every description. Strangled in weeds were heaps of iron and bolts that are now being brought back to life by those who loved and cared about those early railroads. Now you can walk those tracks and rediscover railroading with Don Kirk's Iron Horse Art.

Originally drawn and inked for notecards, stationary, postcards, T-shirts, and art prints back in the early 1990's, this is the first reproduction of some of those works of Pen & Ink art that you can use for coloring.

Don Kirk has been fascinated with railroading ever since he found his first Lionel train set under the Christmas tree at age 10. In Junior High he was building his first HO scale railroad on a 4 x 8 sheet of plywood he set up in his mother's tiny living room. Scenery, lichen, and sawdust engulfed her room. When he went off to college to study architecture, he had to sell his whole layout with its "miles" of track in ovals and figure-eights and oodles of green plastic scenery packed on just 32 square feet of plywood. You can bet his mother was glad to see it go.

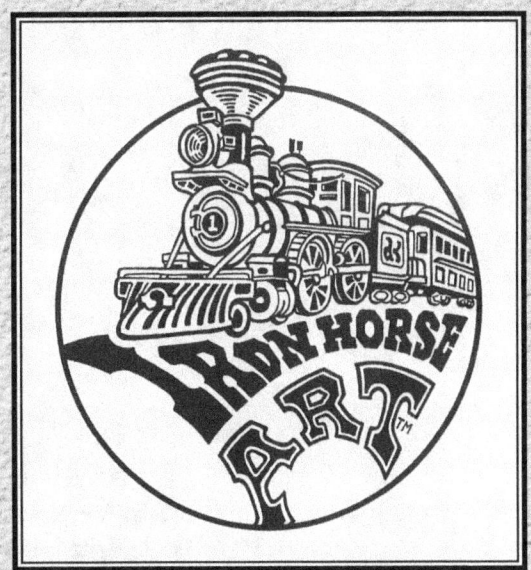

This 1872 Virginia & Truckee 4-4-0 Built By Baldwin Locomotive Works And Labeled The "Reno" Is Currently Located At The Old Tucson Movie Studio Near Tucson, Arizona. The Set Was Built In 1939 For The Movie "Arizona" And Has Been Used For The Filming Of Numerous Movies And Television Westerns Ever Since. They Include "Gunfight At The O.K. Corral," "Rio Bravo," And The "Little House On The Prairie" Television Series.

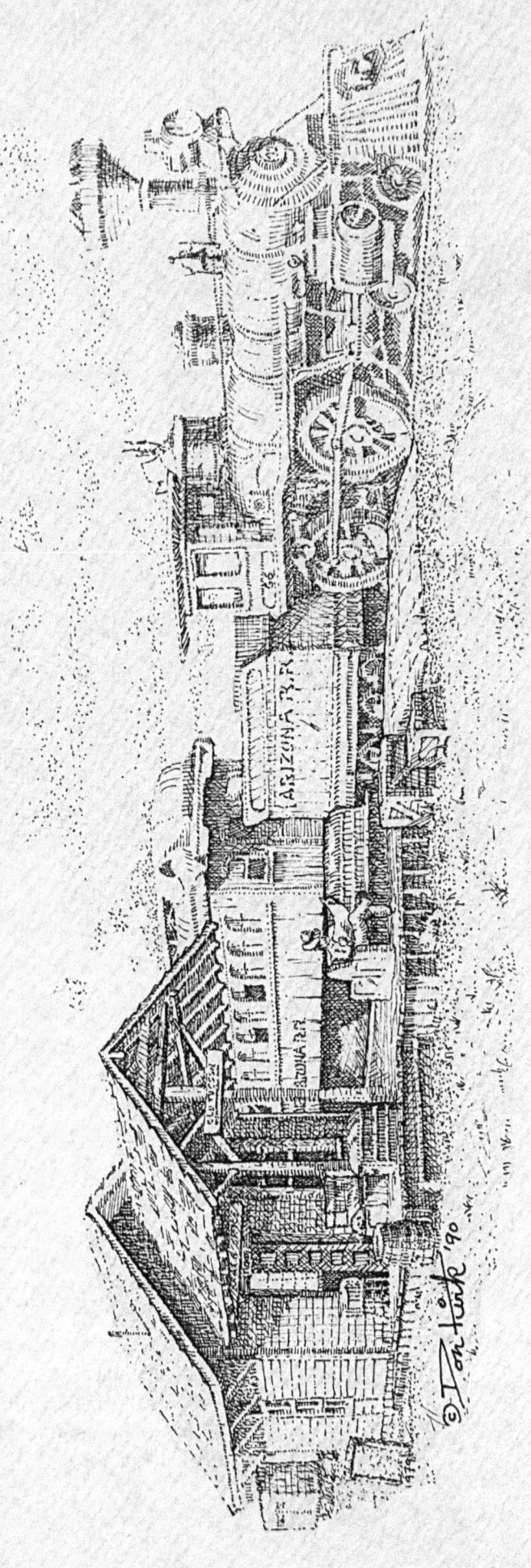

Locomotive No. 206 And No. 94 On The Former Denver, South Park, And Pacific Narrow Gauge Railroad. A 2-6-0 and 1885 2-8-0 with the V&T-Style Sunflower Stacks. In its day the D.S.P. & P. R.R. Running Across The Continental Divide was known as the "The Damn Slow Pulling and Pretty Rough Riding" Line Because Of The Extreme Conditions It Had To Fight, like Blizzards, Rockslides, Floods, And Frequent Derailments.

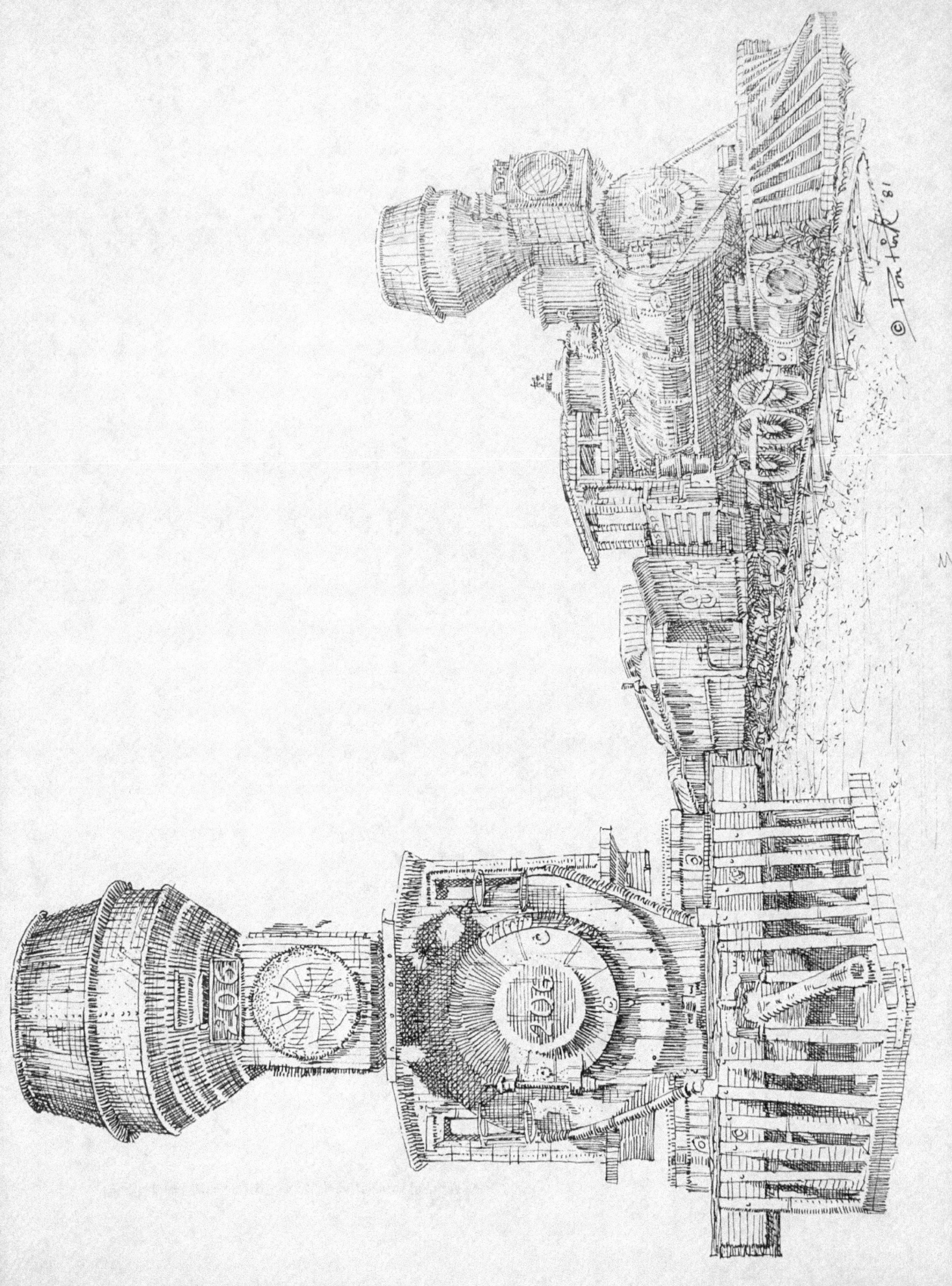

Detail of Locomotive No. 206 with its Sunflower Stack.

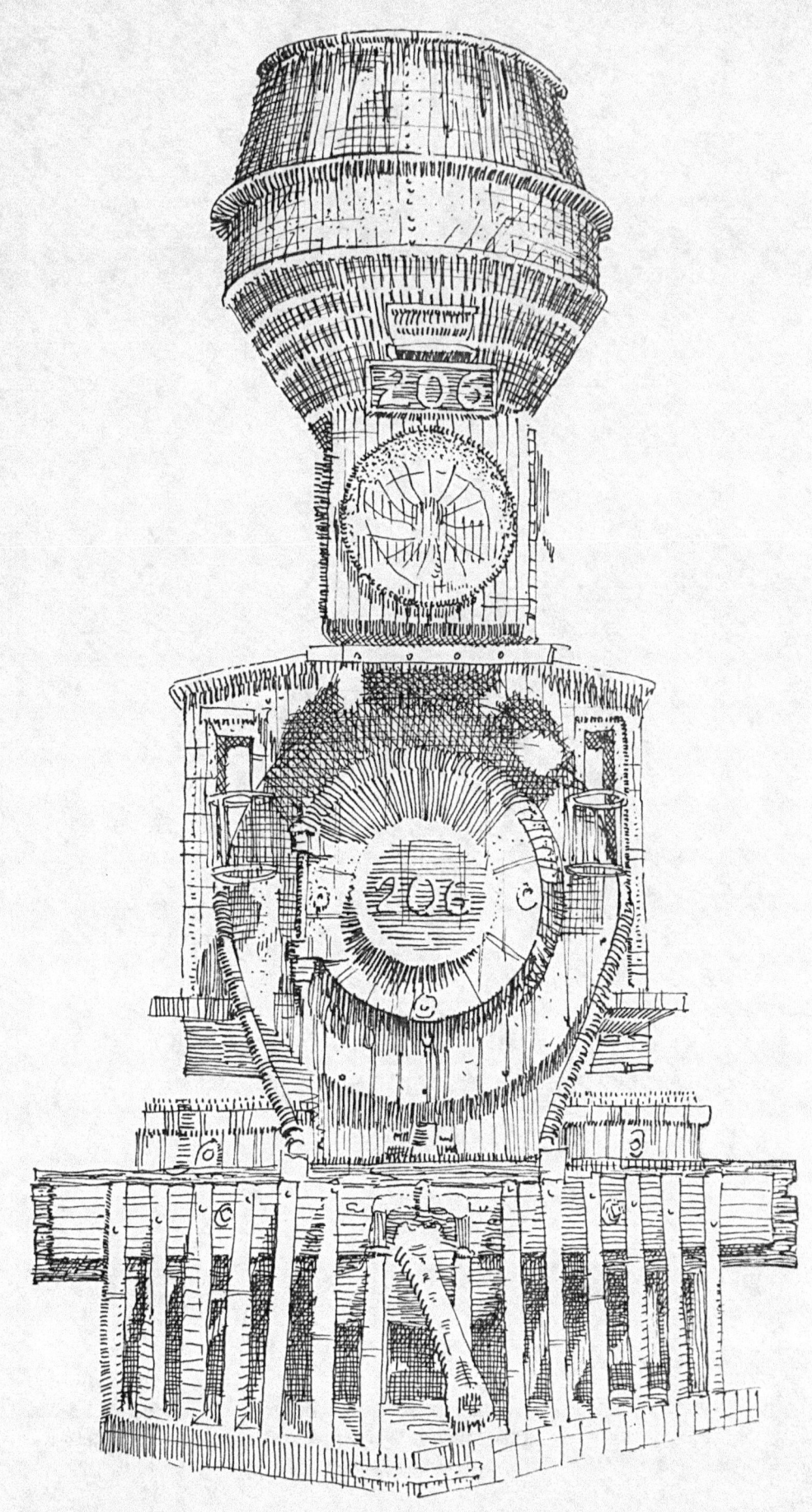

The Oldest Locomotive In Colorado, No. 191, Is A Baldwin 2-8-0 Built In January 1880. It Ran On The Denver, Leadville And Gunnison And Is Currently Located At The Colorado Railroad Museum.

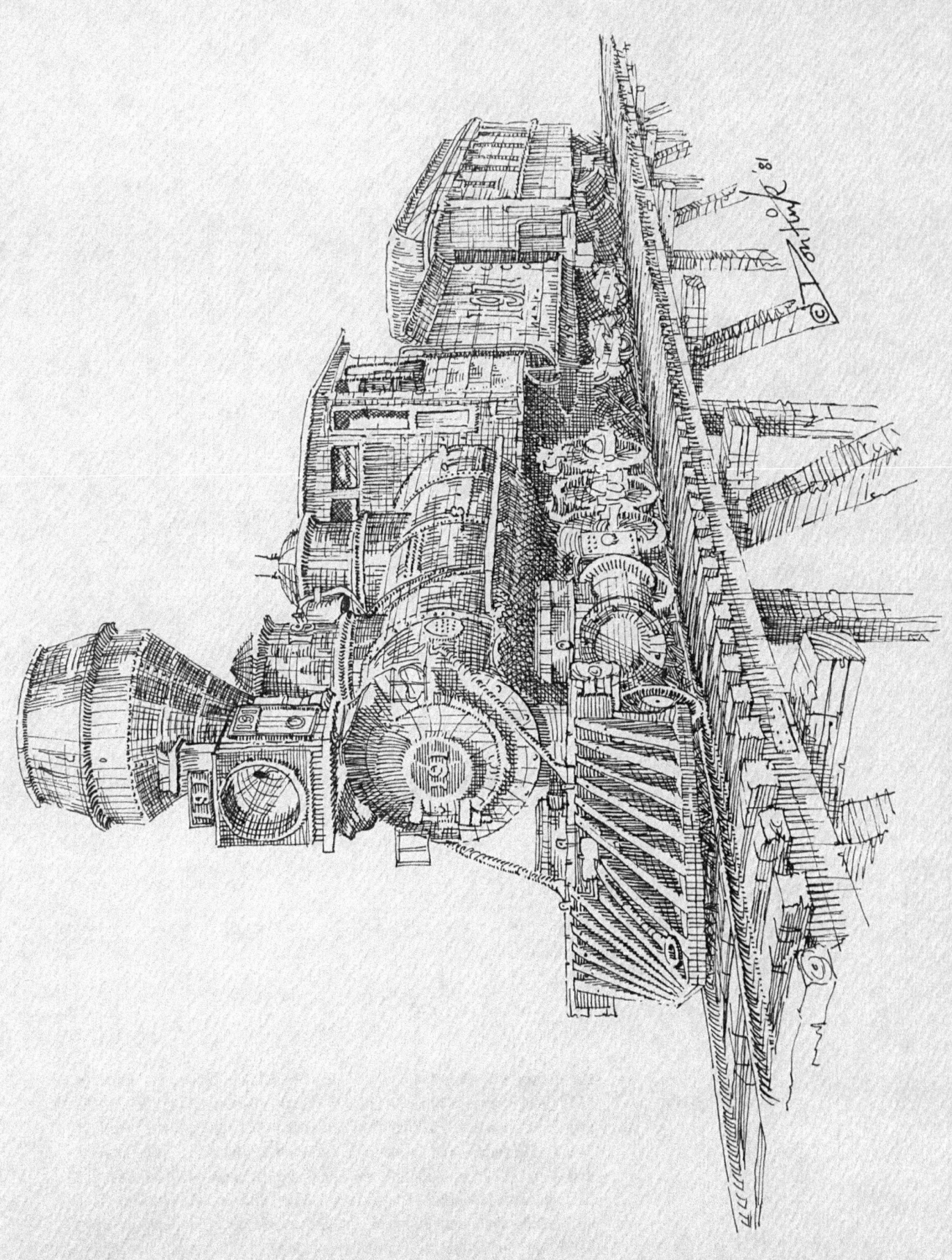

The Virginia & Truckee 4-4-0, No. 11, Built By Baldwin Locomotive Works In 1872, Was Purchased By MGM In 1947 Where It Remained Until Sold To "Old Tucson," Arizona In 1970. With The Photogenic V&T-Style "Sunflower" Stack, It Was Used In Hundreds Of Commercials And Westerns Including "How The West Was Won," "The Cheyenne Social Club," And "Posse." Originally A Woodburner, She Was Converted To Coal In 1886 And Then To Oil In 1905. Her Cylinders Are 16X24 Inches, Boiler Pressure: 130 Pounds, Driver Diameter: 57 Inches, Engine Weight: 65,000 Lbs. And A Traction Effort Calculated To Be 11,920 Pounds.

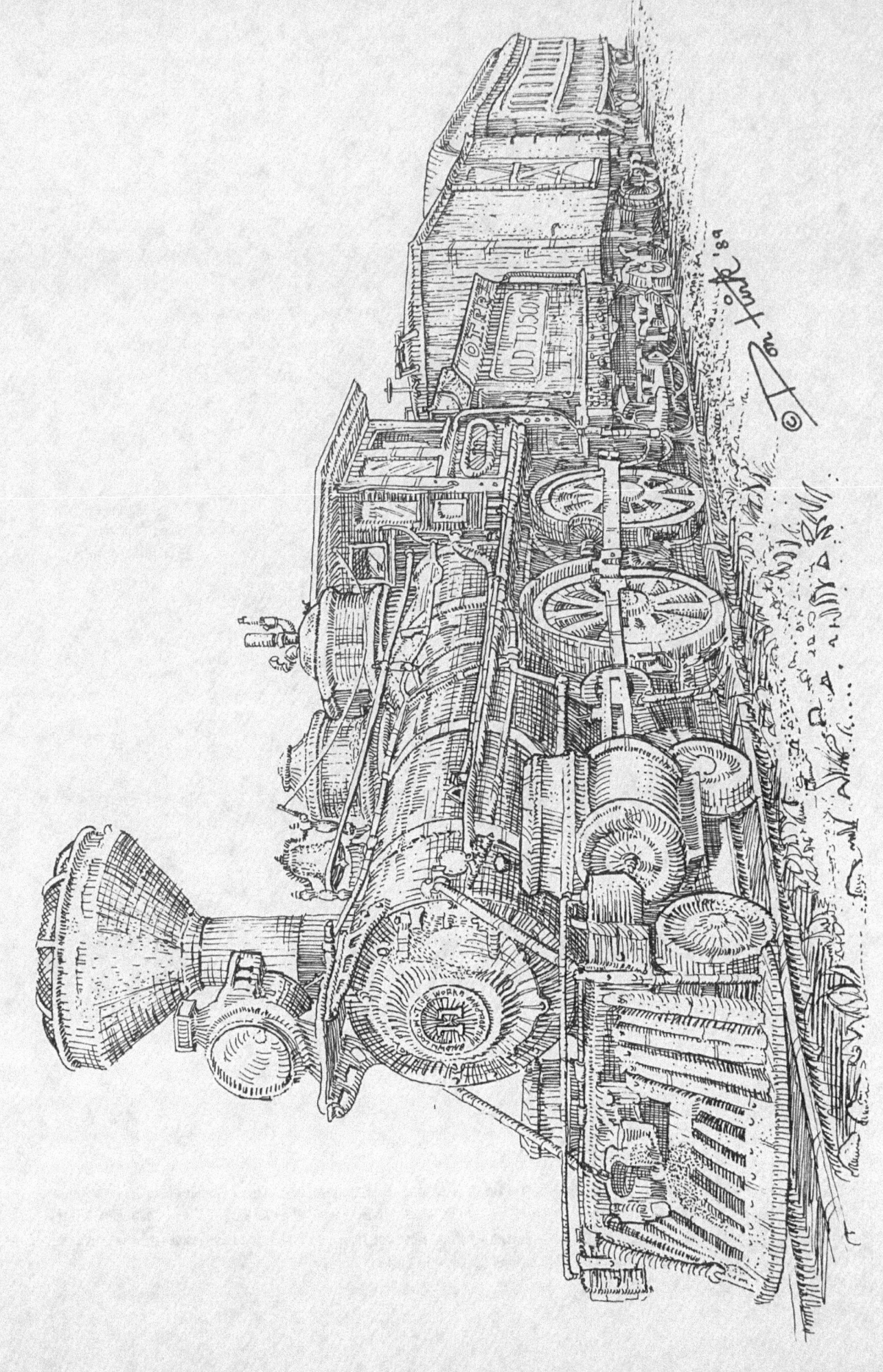

Engine No. 1, The "Mary & Elizabeth, Too," A 2-6-2 Prairie Class Steam Locomotive Was Built By The Baldwin Locomotive Works. The Waco, Beaumont, Trinity & Sabine Railroad Acquired It In 1949. It Currently Resides At The Galveston Railroad Museum In Texas.

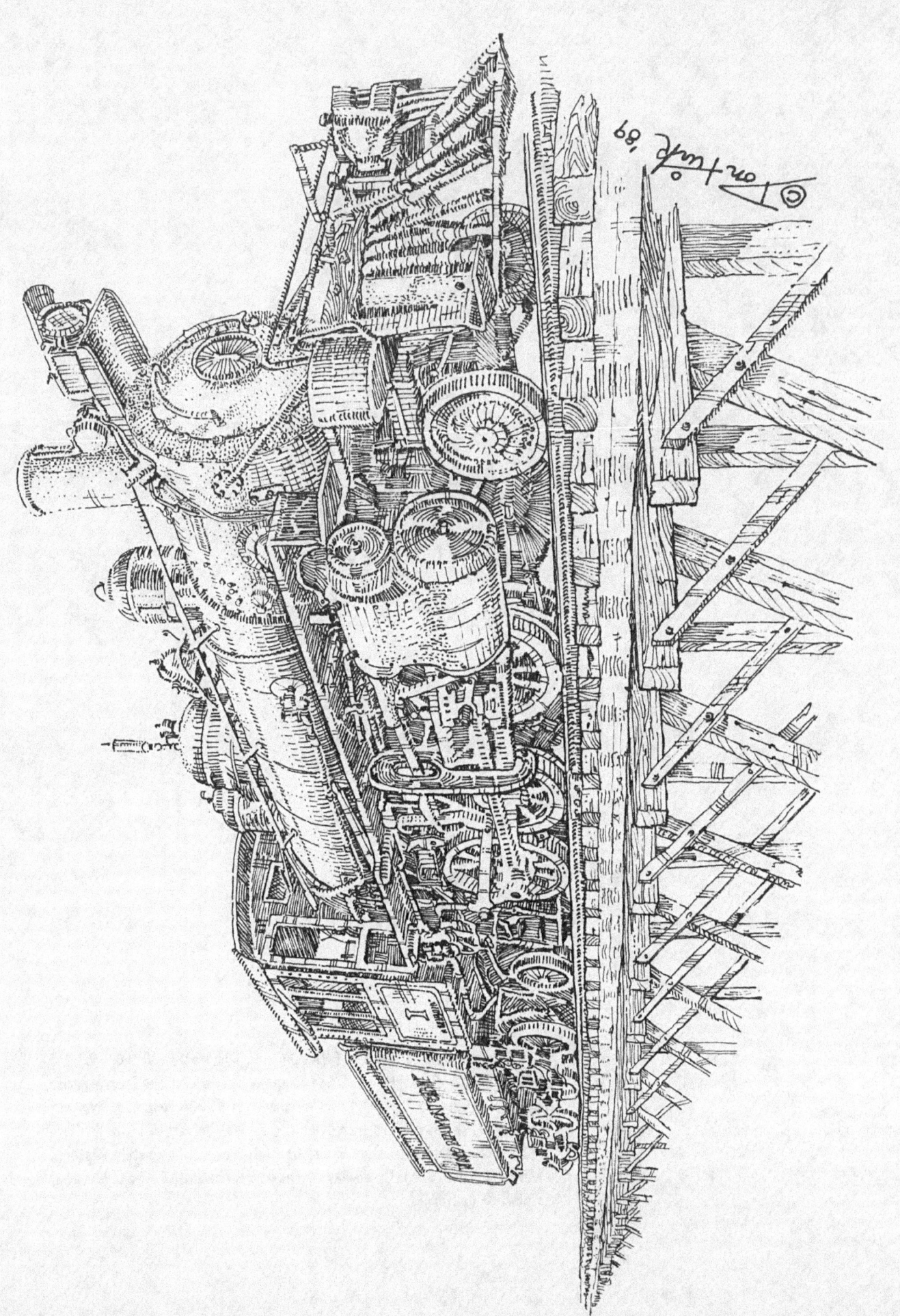

The "C. P. Huntington," A Tiny 4-2-4 Woodburning Locomotive With One Driving Axle, Was Built By Danforth, Cook, And Company In 1863 For The Central Pacific Lines. It Was Only 29-Feet Long And Weighed Just 39,000 Pounds. A Standard Gauge Engine, She Has 11X15-Inch Cylinders, 54 Inch Drivers, A Boiler Pressure Of 110 Pounds, And A Traction Effort Of 3,510 Pounds. Completely Restored To Mint Condition, She Is On Display At The California State Railroad Museum, Sacramento, California.

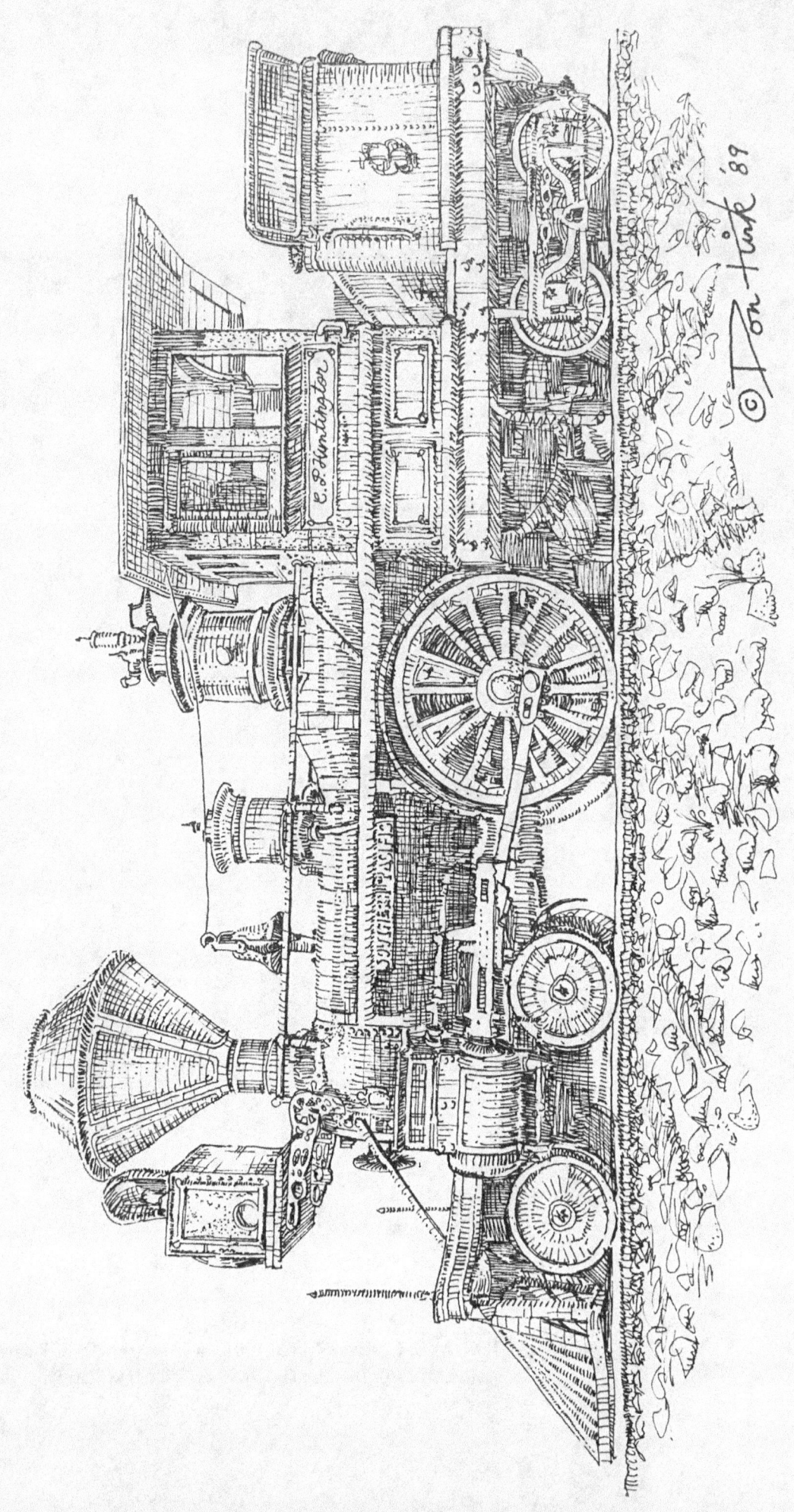

No. 1744, A 2-6-0 Baldwin Built In 1901, An Ex-Southern Pacific Railroad
Locomotive, Is Now On The Heber Creeper Scenic Railroad At Heber City, Utah.

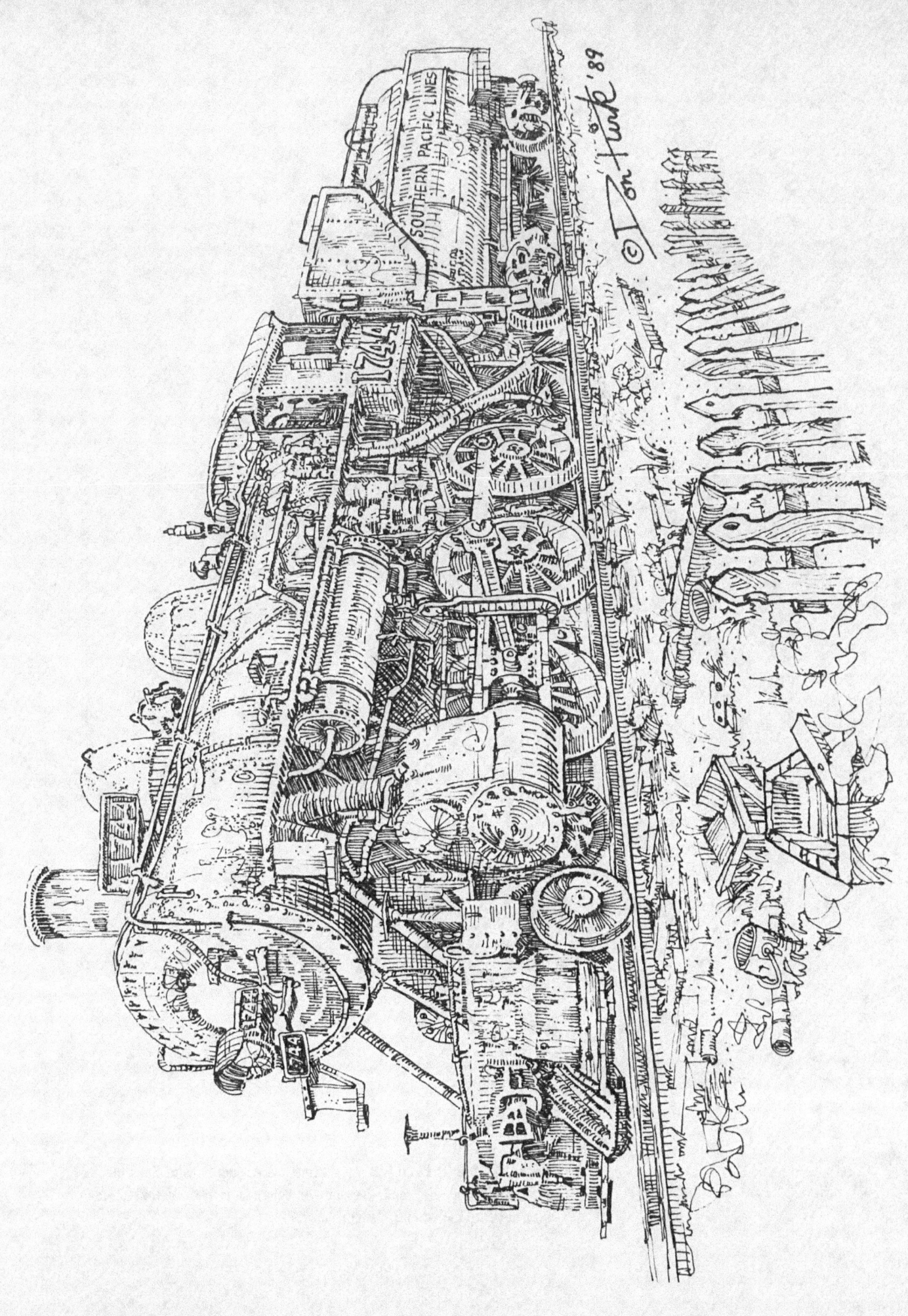

No. 40, A 2-8-0 Of 1920 Baldwin Vintage, Once Made Regular Runs On The Georgetown Loop Railroad, Georgetown, Colorado. It Was Purchased From International Railways Of Central America.

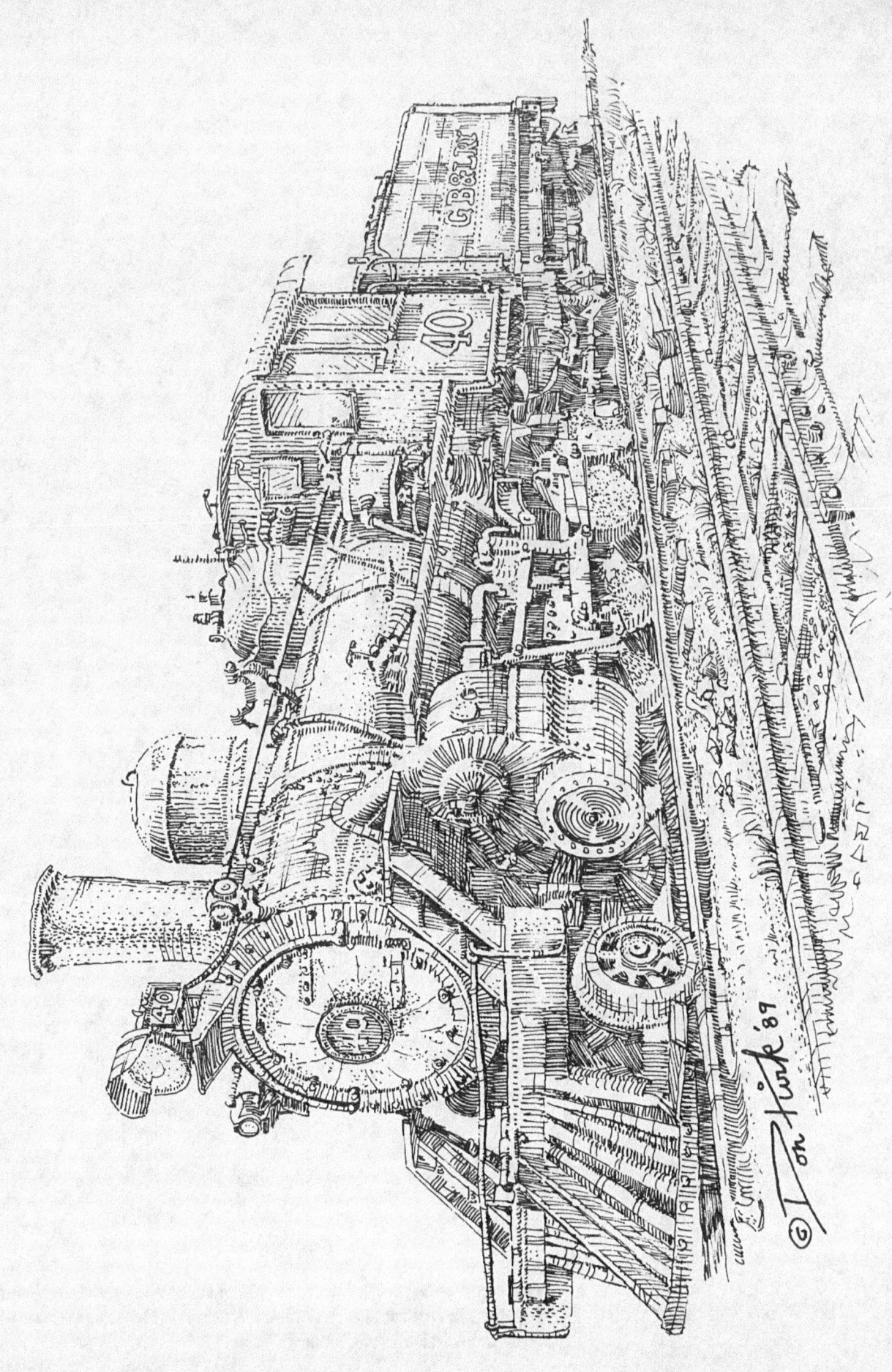

This Depot Was Built In San Saba, Texas In 1911 By The Gulf, Colorado And Santa Fe Railway Co. Originally Constructed As A Freight Depot Because The Passenger Depot Was A Separate Brick Building.

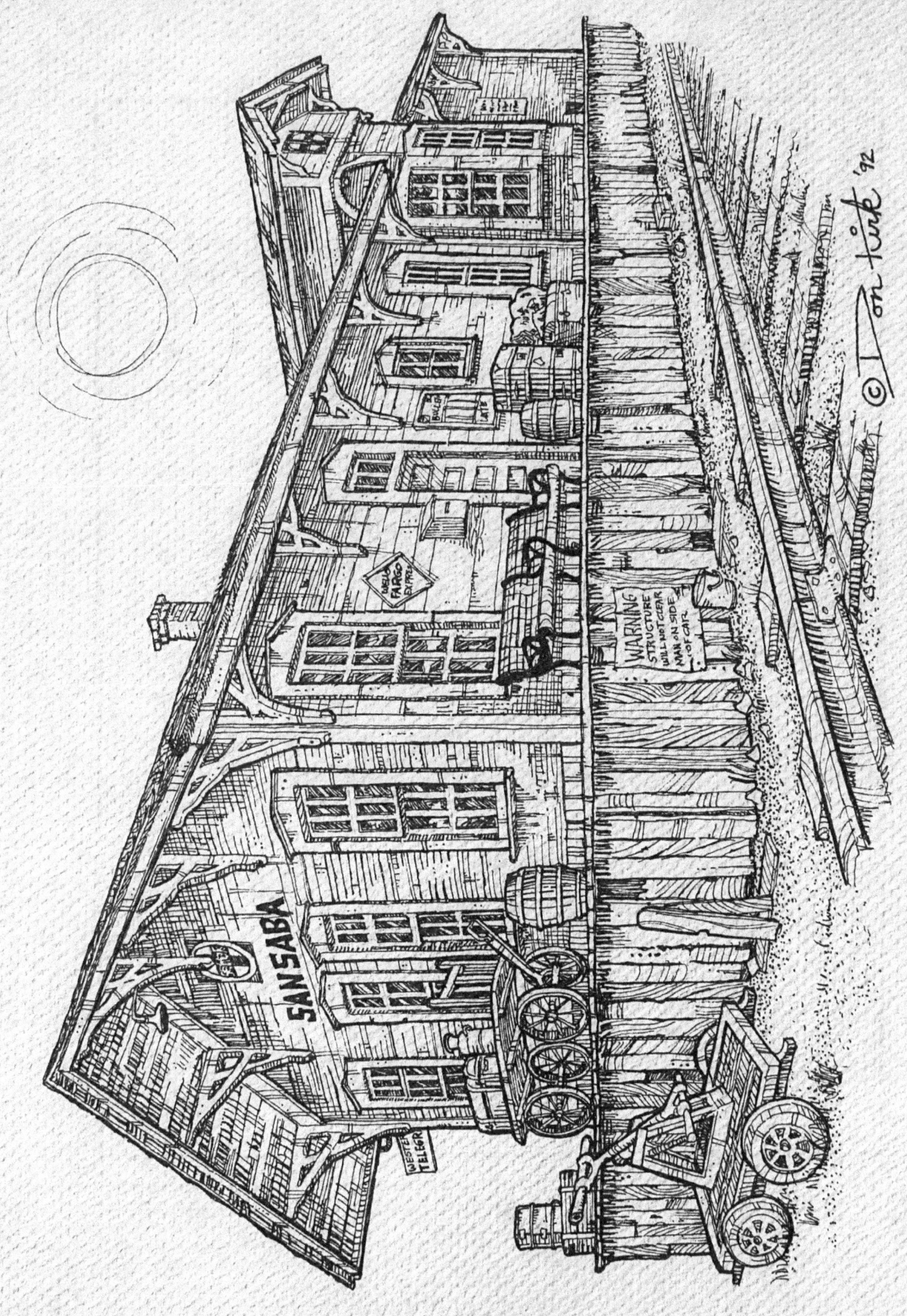

WHAT'S WHAT
ON THE 'MY HEART BELONGS TO RAILROADING' T-SHIRT:

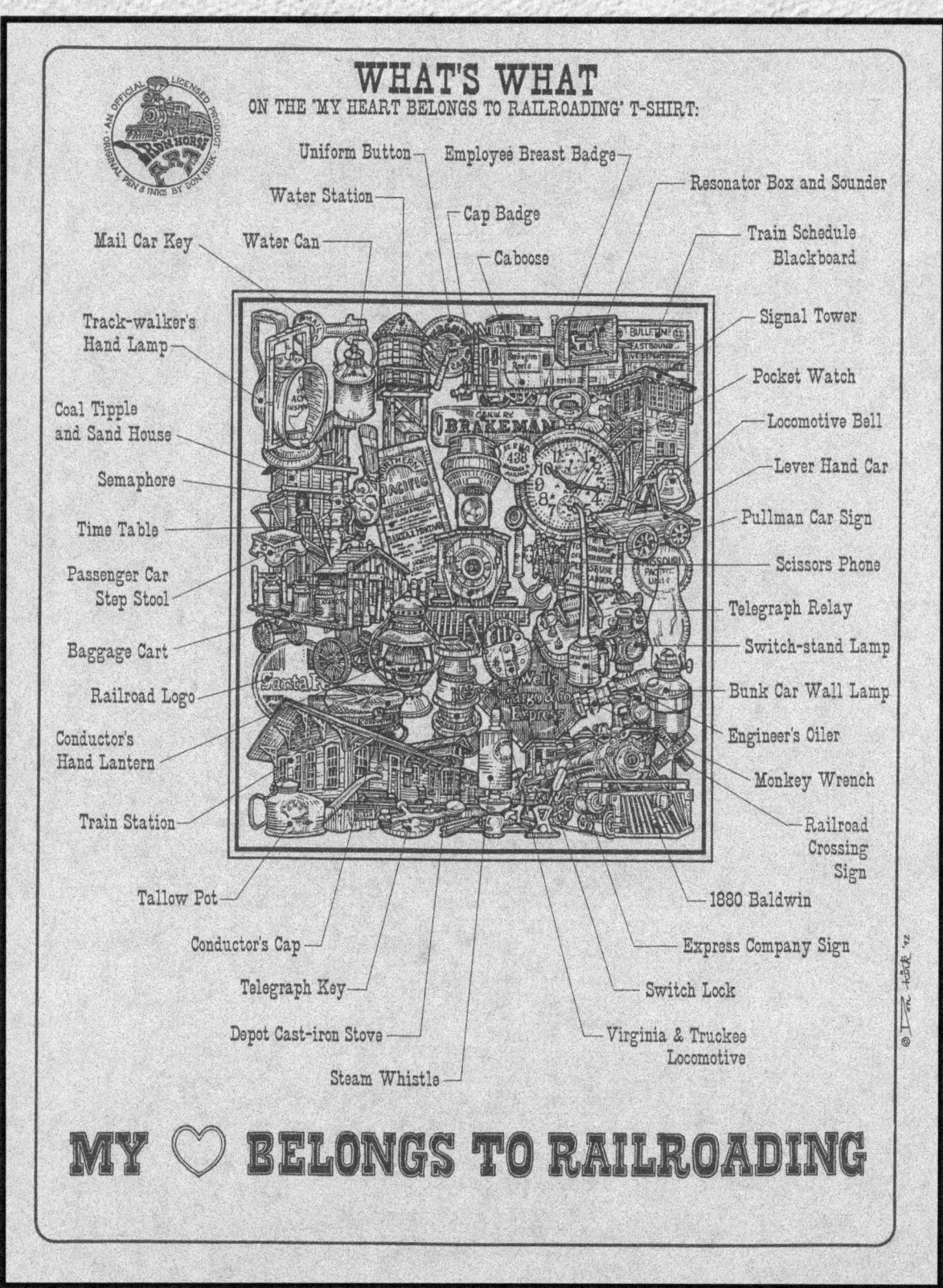

Uniform Button
Employee Breast Badge
Resonator Box and Sounder
Water Station
Cap Badge
Train Schedule Blackboard
Mail Car Key
Water Can
Caboose
Signal Tower
Track-walker's Hand Lamp
Pocket Watch
Coal Tipple and Sand House
Locomotive Bell
Semaphore
Lever Hand Car
Time Table
Pullman Car Sign
Passenger Car Step Stool
Scissors Phone
Telegraph Relay
Baggage Cart
Switch-stand Lamp
Railroad Logo
Bunk Car Wall Lamp
Conductor's Hand Lantern
Engineer's Oiler
Monkey Wrench
Train Station
Railroad Crossing Sign
Tallow Pot
1880 Baldwin
Conductor's Cap
Express Company Sign
Telegraph Key
Switch Lock
Depot Cast-iron Stove
Virginia & Truckee Locomotive
Steam Whistle

MY ♡ BELONGS TO RAILROADING

A T-Shirt Design: Montage Of Railroadiana: The Artifacts That Made It Possible To Move Passengers And Freight Across These United States.

MY ♡ BELONGS

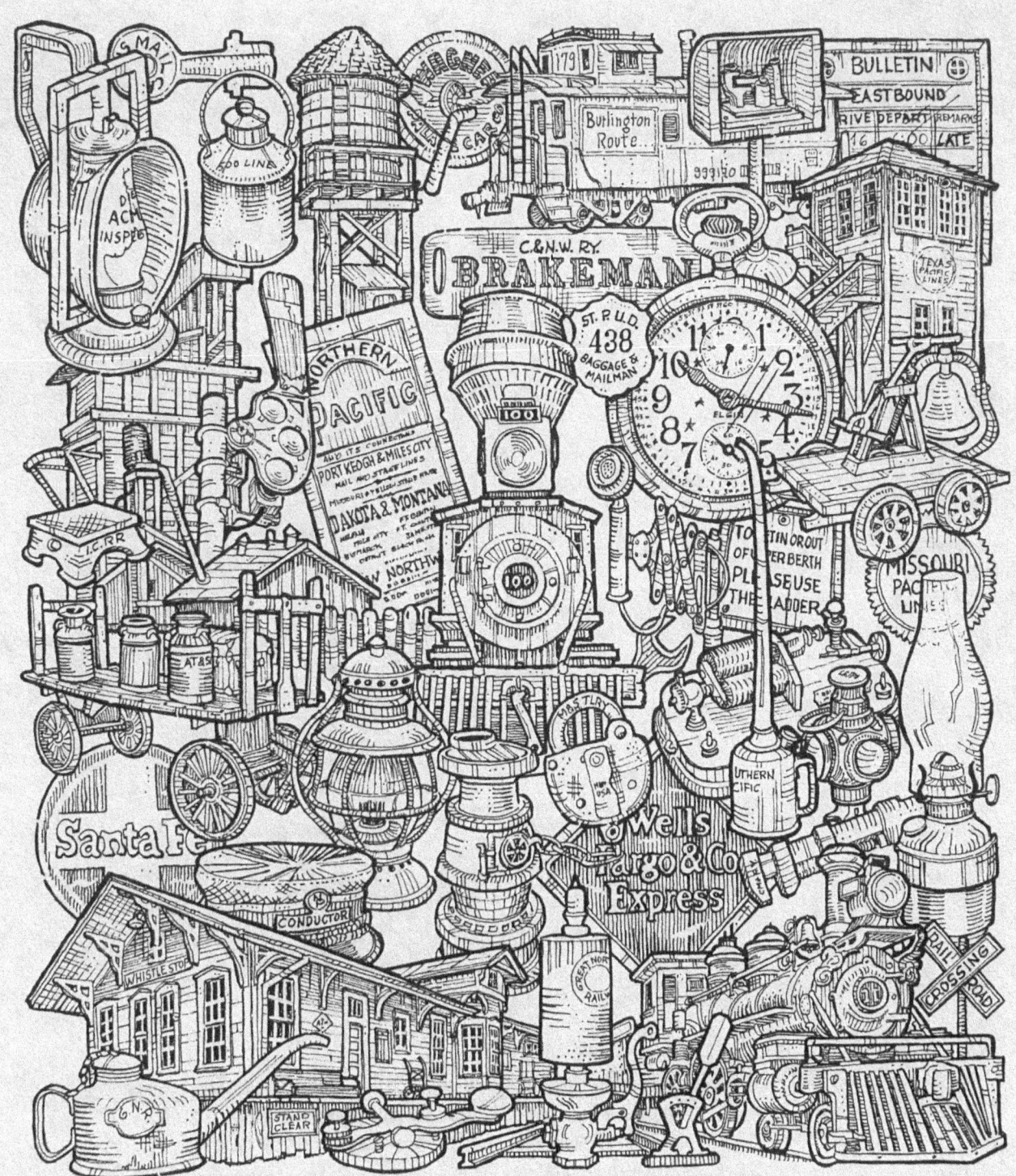

TO RAILROADING

Sitting At The Central City Station Is Number "71," An 1896, 2-8-0 Baldwin Locomotive With It's Unique Ridgeway Spark Arrestor. She Is Coal-Fired And Weighs 80,500 Pounds. Built By Burnham, Williams & Co., Her Cylinders Are 15-1/2 X 20 Inch, Boiler Pressure Rides At 180 Pounds, And With 37-Inch Drivers And An Engine Weight Of 80,500, The Traction Effort Comes To 19,848 Lbs. Formerly On The Colorado & Southern Railroad, She Is Now Running On The Black Hawk & Central City Narrow Gauge Railroad In Central City, Colorado.

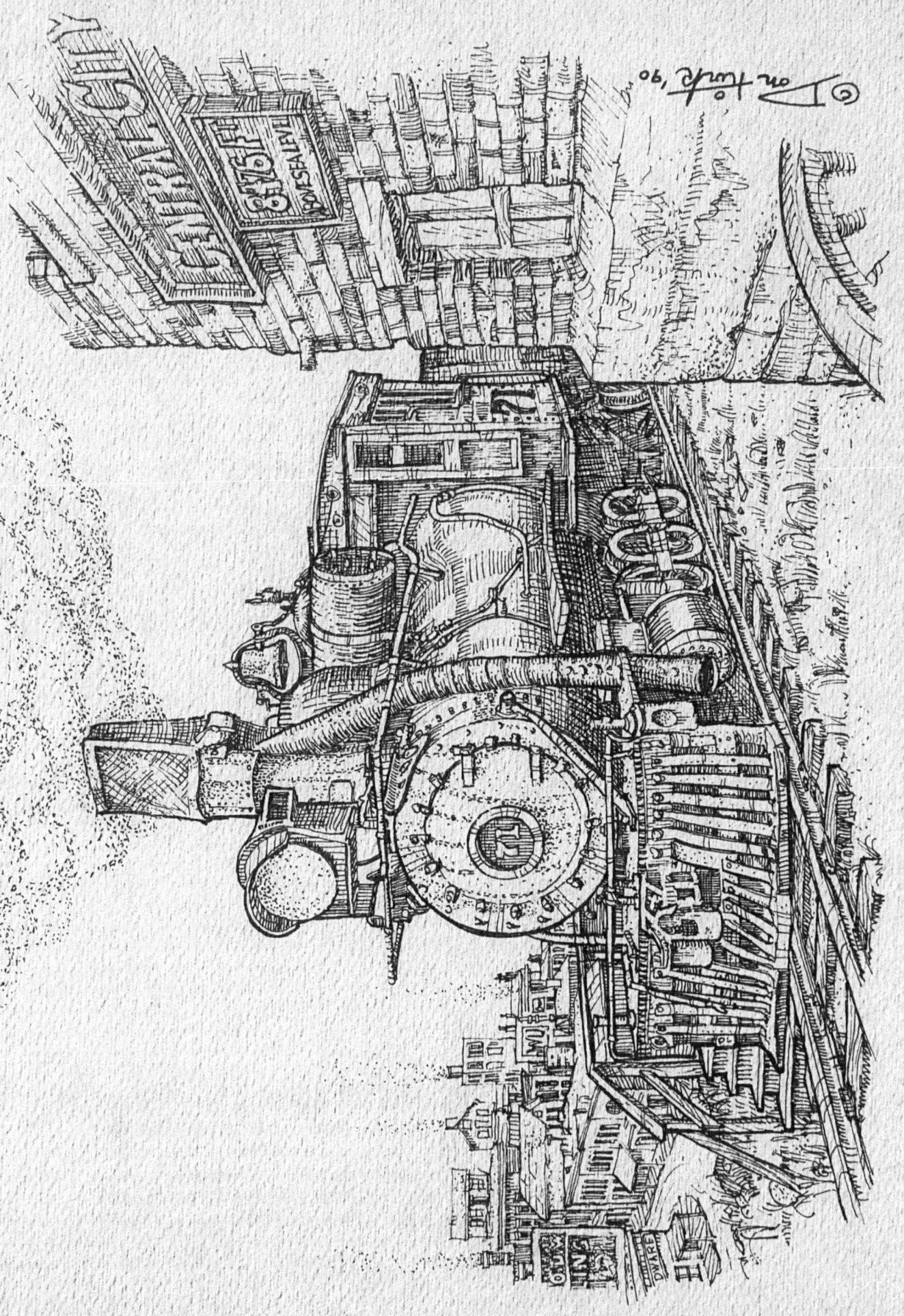

Number "583" Pauses At An 1880'S Style Masonry Railroad Depot At The Colorado Railroad Museum In Golden, Colorado. The Locomotive Is A Class C-28, 2-8-0 Baldwin Built In 1890 For The Denver And Rio Grande. Over 100 Of These Locomotives Were Built In 1888 Thru 1892 For Freight Service On The New Standard Gauge Denver-Pueblo-Ogden Line. With A Weight Of 113,200 Pounds, 46-Inch Drivers, 20X24 Cylinders, And A Boiler Pressure Of 140 Pounds, The "583" Produces A Traction Effort Of 24,900 Pounds.

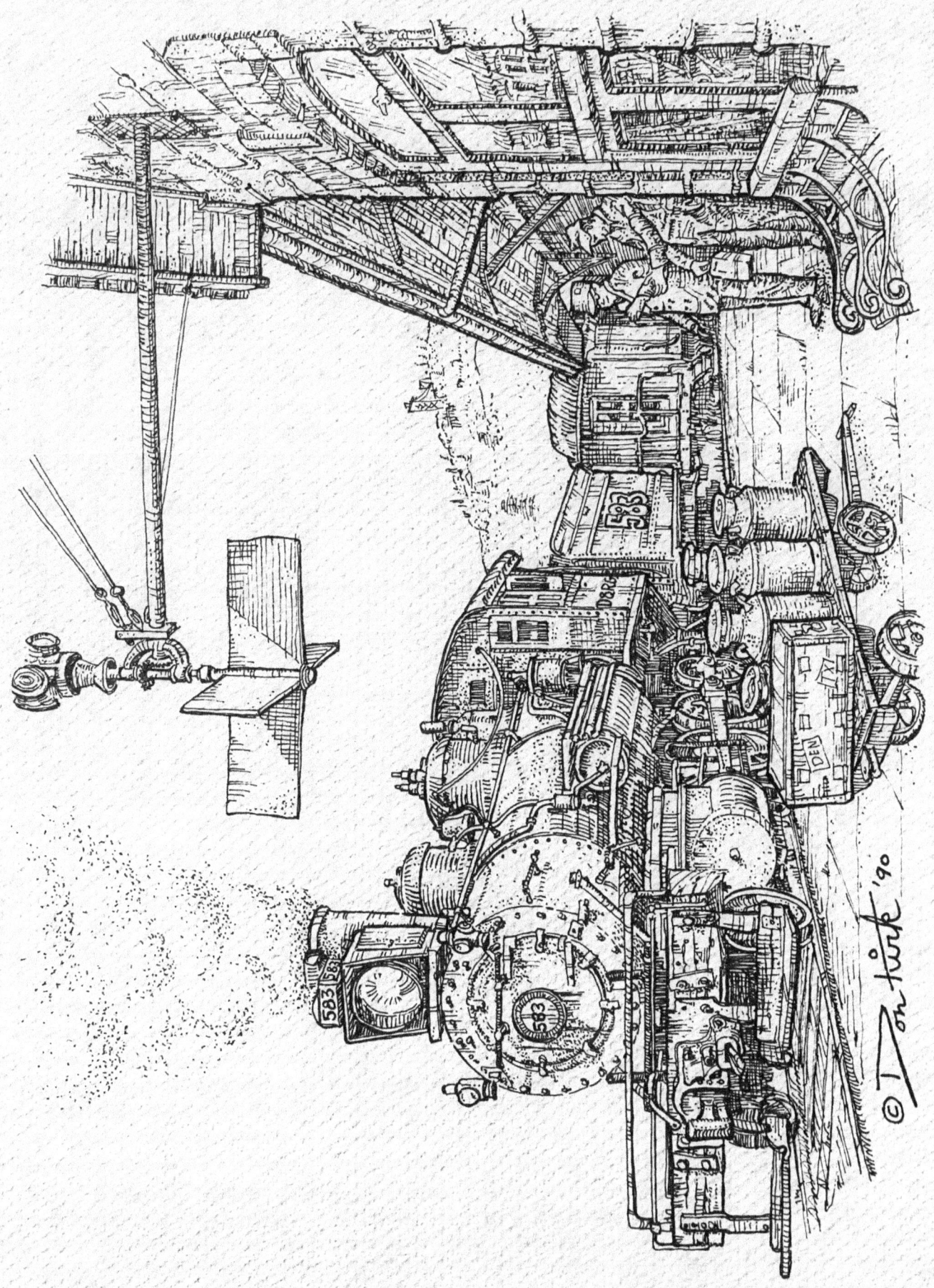

Water Tank And Pumphouse To Fill The Engine Tender While Passengers Load And Disembark From The Nearby Train Station. A Well Was Dug Here To Retrieve Inexpensive Water.

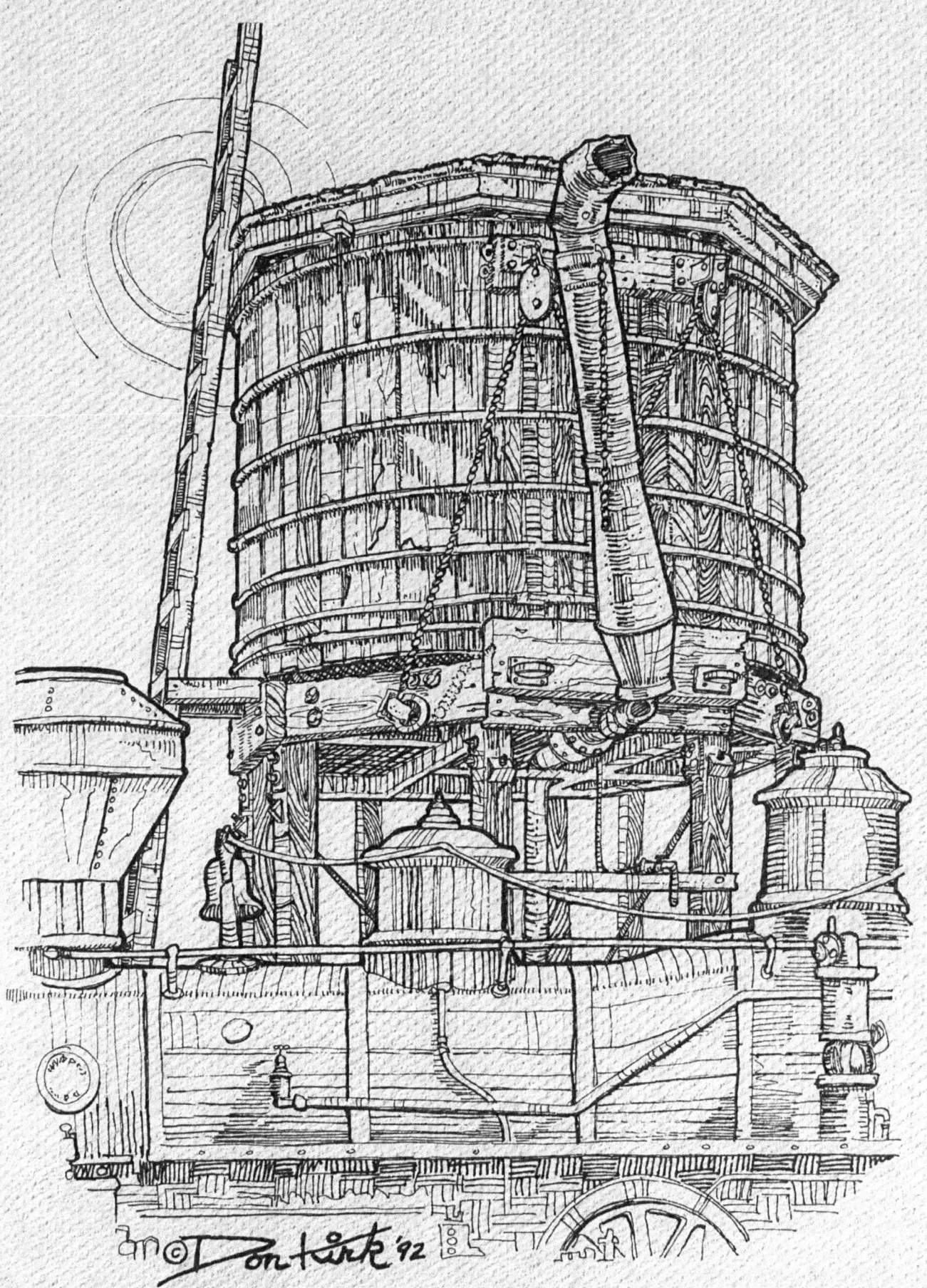

© Don Kirk '92

The 1907 International And Great Northern Railway Station, San Antonio, Texas—Later The Missouri Pacific Depot—Is In Cattleman's Square Near The Former Union Stockyards. Currently, The Station Is Used As An AMTRAK And Commuter Station For Bus, Light Rail, And Street Car. The Architect, Harvey L. Page Imitated The Area's Spanish Missions In His Design. The Copper Dome Extending Eighty-Eight Feet Into The Air Has A Bronze Statue Of An Indian Shooting An Arrow.

It Was In 1877 That Rail Service First Came To San Antonio, Texas And In 1903 The Southern Pacific Railway Station Was Built. It Became Know As The "Sunset Station" Honoring The New Orleans To Los Angeles Rail Route It Served. The Station Was Designed By Southern Pacific Personnel Led By Architect John D. Isaacs Who Adapted The Alamo's Mission Style.

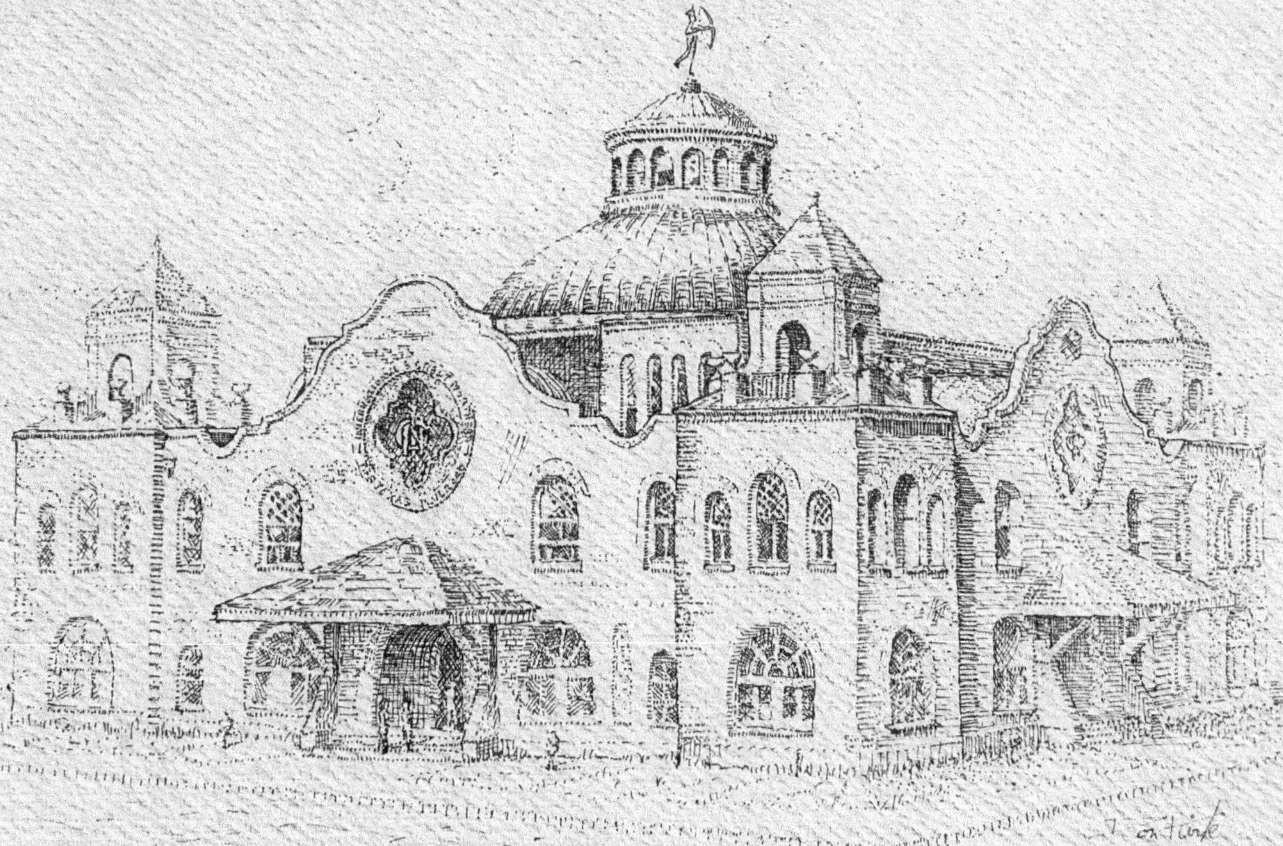

INTERNATIONAL & GREAT NORTHERN
RAILROAD STATION No7
San Antonio, Texas

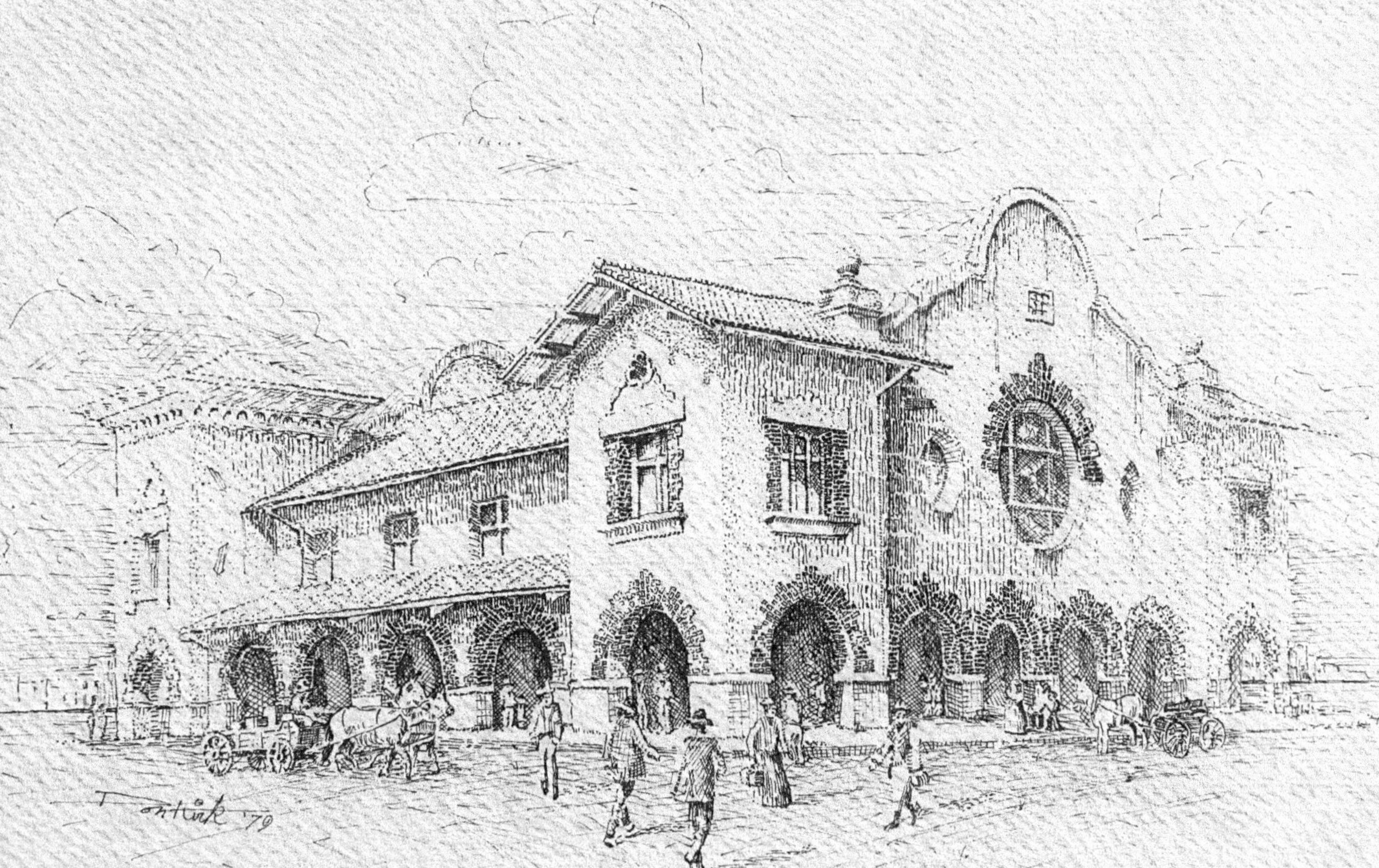

1903
Southern Pacific Railway Station
San Antonio, Texas

Approaching On The Main Line Is Number "500", A 137-Ton, 1911, 4-6-2 Baldwin. An Oil Burner With 73-Inch Drivers And 23-1/2 X 28-Inch Cylinders, She Has A Traction Effort Of 39,650 Lbs. Waiting On The Siding Is Number "400," An 87-Ton, 1917, 2-8-2 Baldwin With 54-Inch Drivers, 21 X 26 Cylinders, And A Traction Effort Rating Of 33,400 Lbs. Both Locomotives Currently Run On The Texas State Railroad Between Palestine And Rusk, Texas.

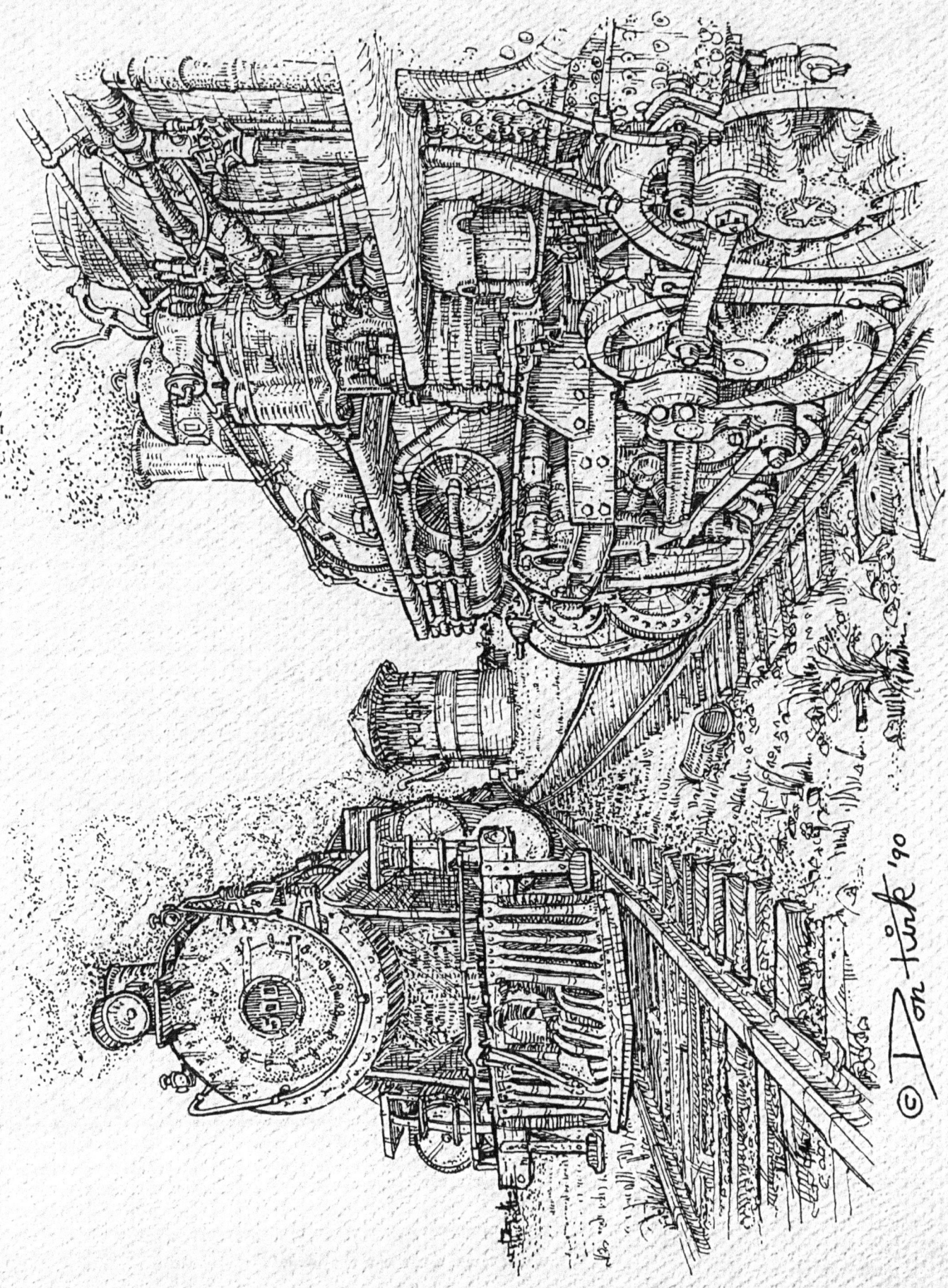

© Don Tuttle '90

Detail Of The 1917, 2-8-2 Baldwin With 54-Inch Drivers, 21 X 26 Cylinders, And A Traction Effort Rating Of 33,400 Pounds.

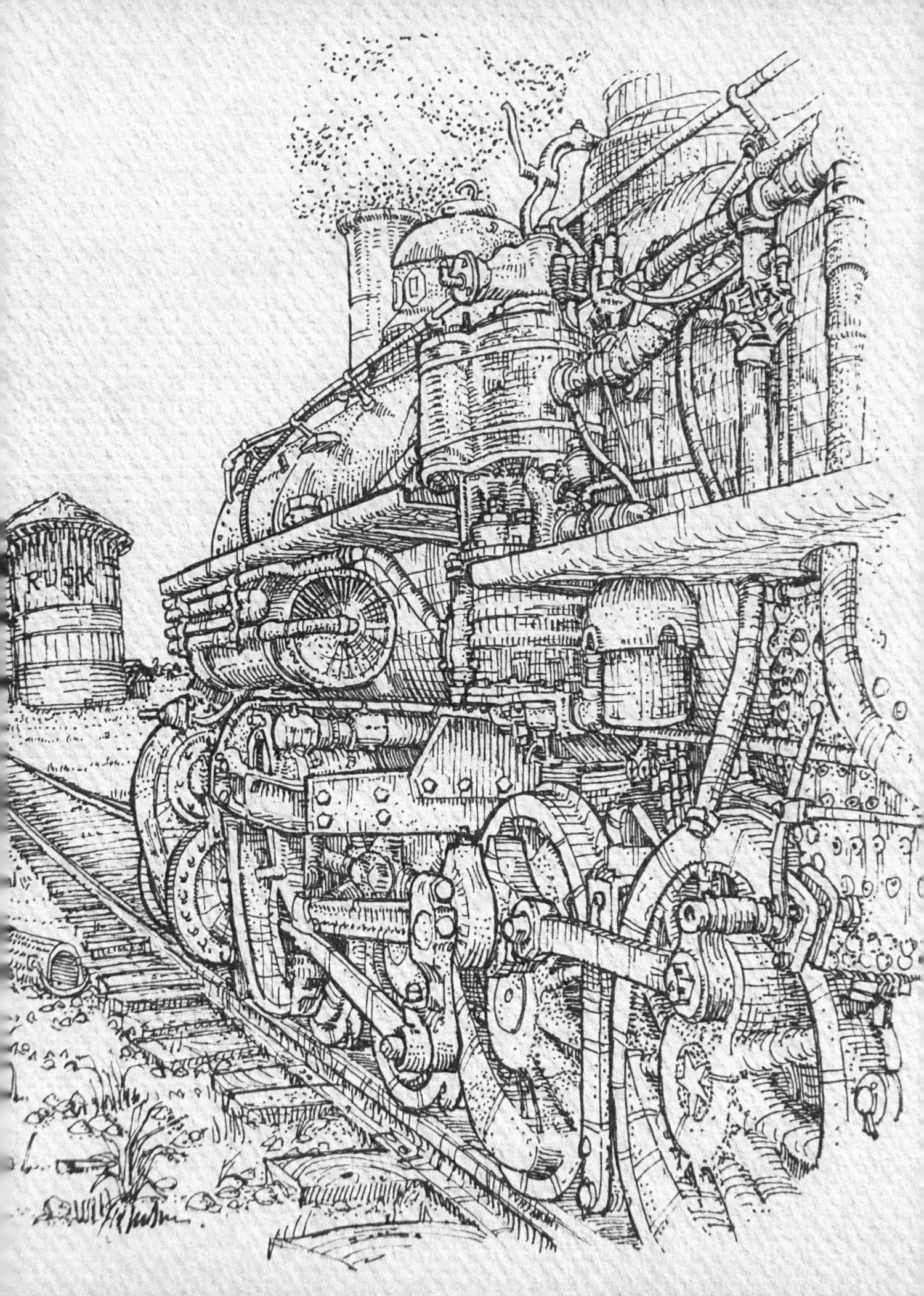

Number "489" A Class K-36, 2-8-2 Steam Locomotive Built In 1925 For The Denver & Rio Grande Western Railroad Co., Pauses For A Refreshing Drink Of Water At The Antonito Water Tank On The Cumbres & Toltec Scenic Railroad, A Spectacular Narrow-Gauge Line That Runs On The Border Between Colorado And New Mexico. This "Old Girl" Is Coal-Fired, Weighs 93-1/2 Tons, And Has A Traction Effort Rated At 36,200 Pounds.

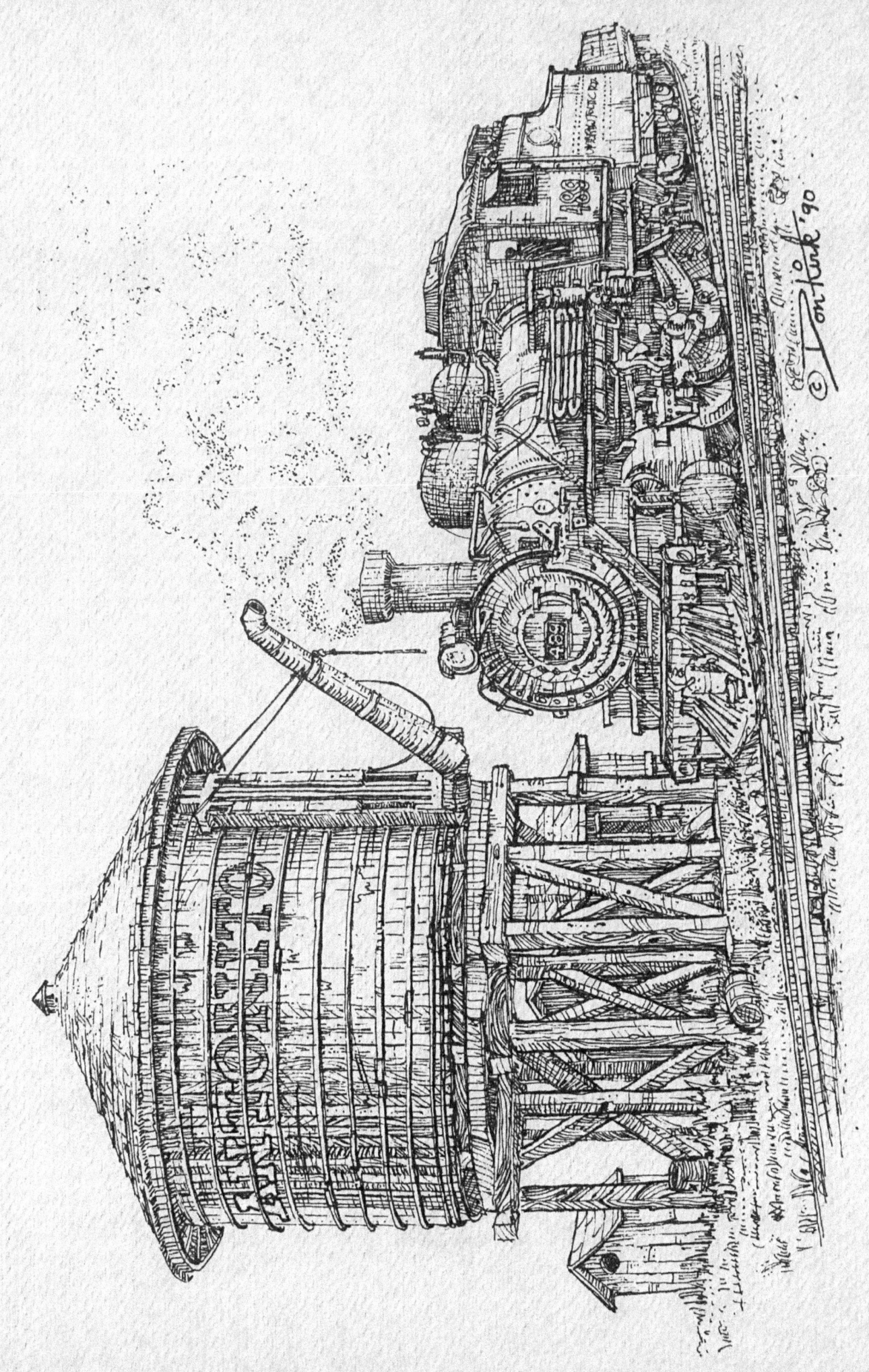

Sitting In An Engine Shed At Felton, California Are Two Geared Locomotives:
An 1899 Heisler On The Right And A 1912 Shay Named "Dixianna" On The
Left. The Shay, Built By The Lima Locomotive Works, Weighs 42 Tons And Has
A Traction Effort Of 17, 330 Pounds. The Heisler Engine, Number "2," Was Built
By Stearns Manufacturing And Weighs 37 Pounds With A Traction Effort Of
14,000 Pounds. Both Engines Do Service On The Roaring Camp And Big Trees
Narrow Gauge Railroad.

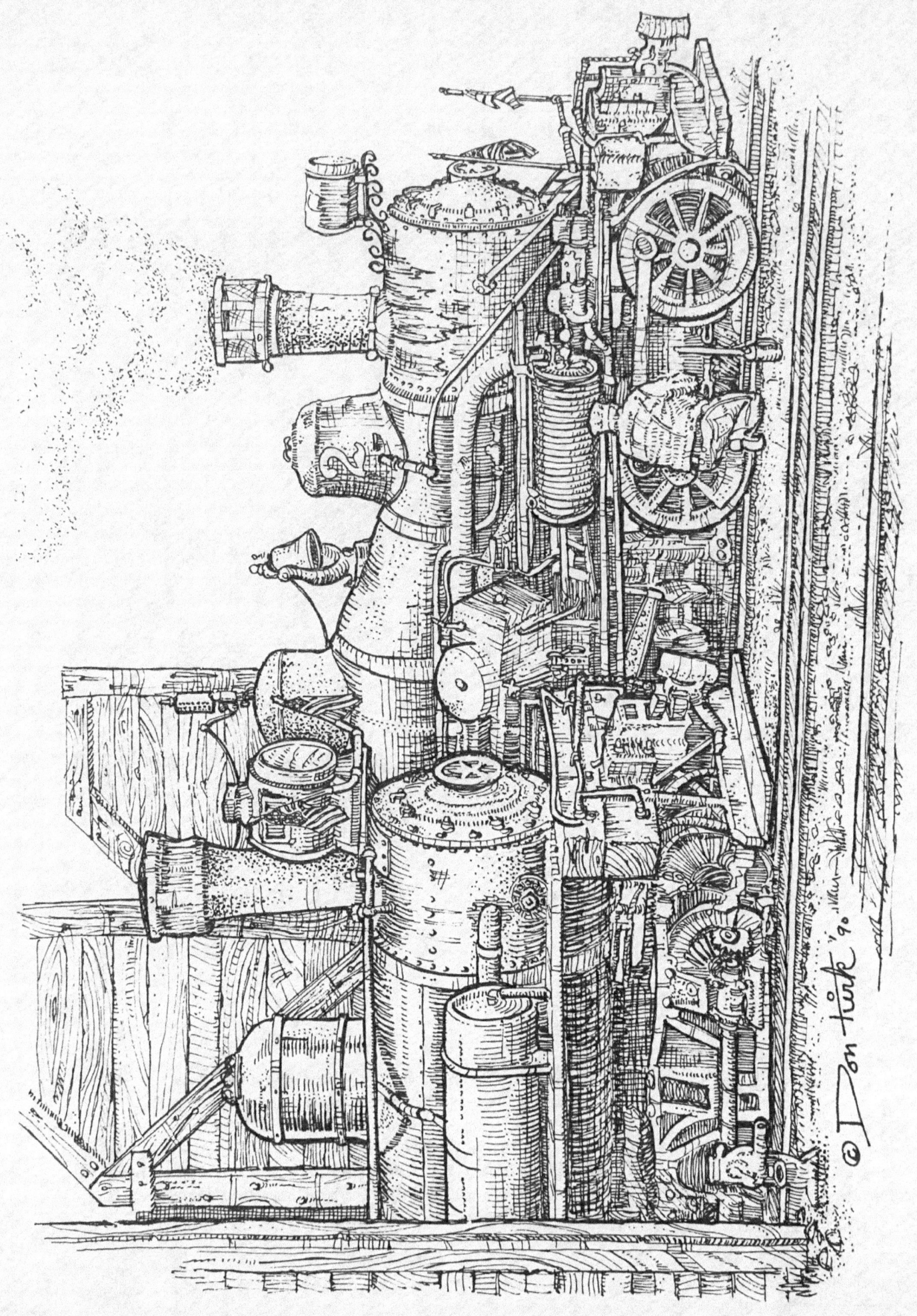

Number "191", A Narrow Gauge 2-8-0 Baldwin Built In 1880, Leaves The "No Agua" Tank At The Colorado Railroad Museum In Golden, Colorado. The "191" Was Originally The Denver, South Park & Pacific Numbered "51," But In 1885 Was Renumbered "191" For The Denver, Leadville & Gunnison. Weighing In At 31 Tons, With 37-Inch Drivers, 15X18 Cylinders, A Boiler Pressure Of 150 Pounds, And A Traction Effort Of 13900 Pounds, It Is The Oldest Locomotive In Colorado And The Only Surviving Locomotive Of The Original D. S. P. & P.

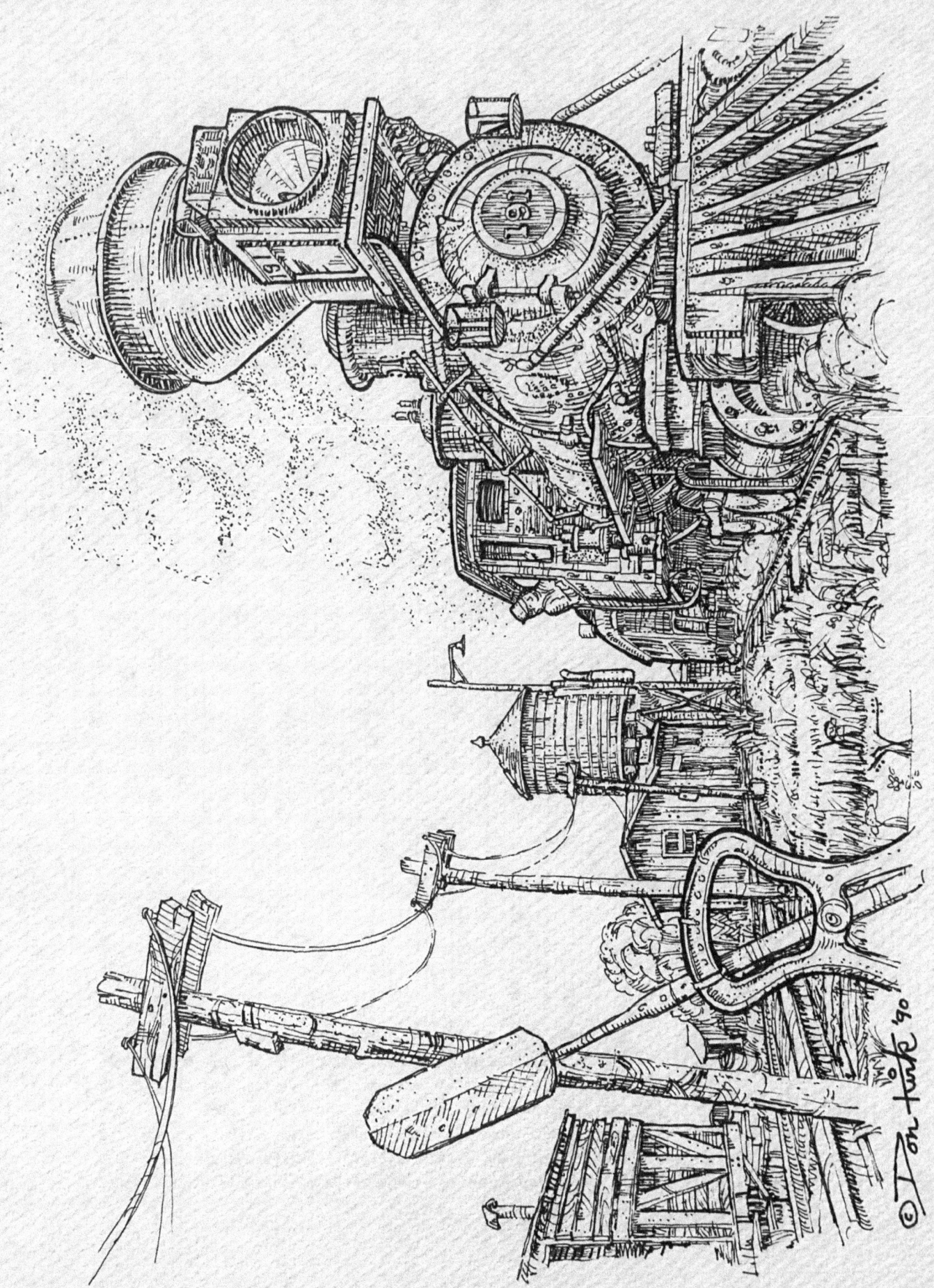

This Two-Truck Heisler, Number "2," Is A Geared Steam Locomotive Built By Sterns Manufacturing Company In Erie, Pennsylvania For The Hetch, Hetchy & Yosemite Railroad In 1899. Favored By Lumbermen, The Heisler Could Haul Heavy Loads Up Steep Grades And Around Tight Mountain Curves Without Flinching. She Weighs In At 37 Tons, Produces 200 Pounds Of Steam Pressure And Has A Traction Effort Of 14,000 Pounds. The "Toulumne" Is The World's Oldest Operating Heisler And Runs On The Roaring Damp And Big Trees Narrow Gauge Railroad In Felton, California.

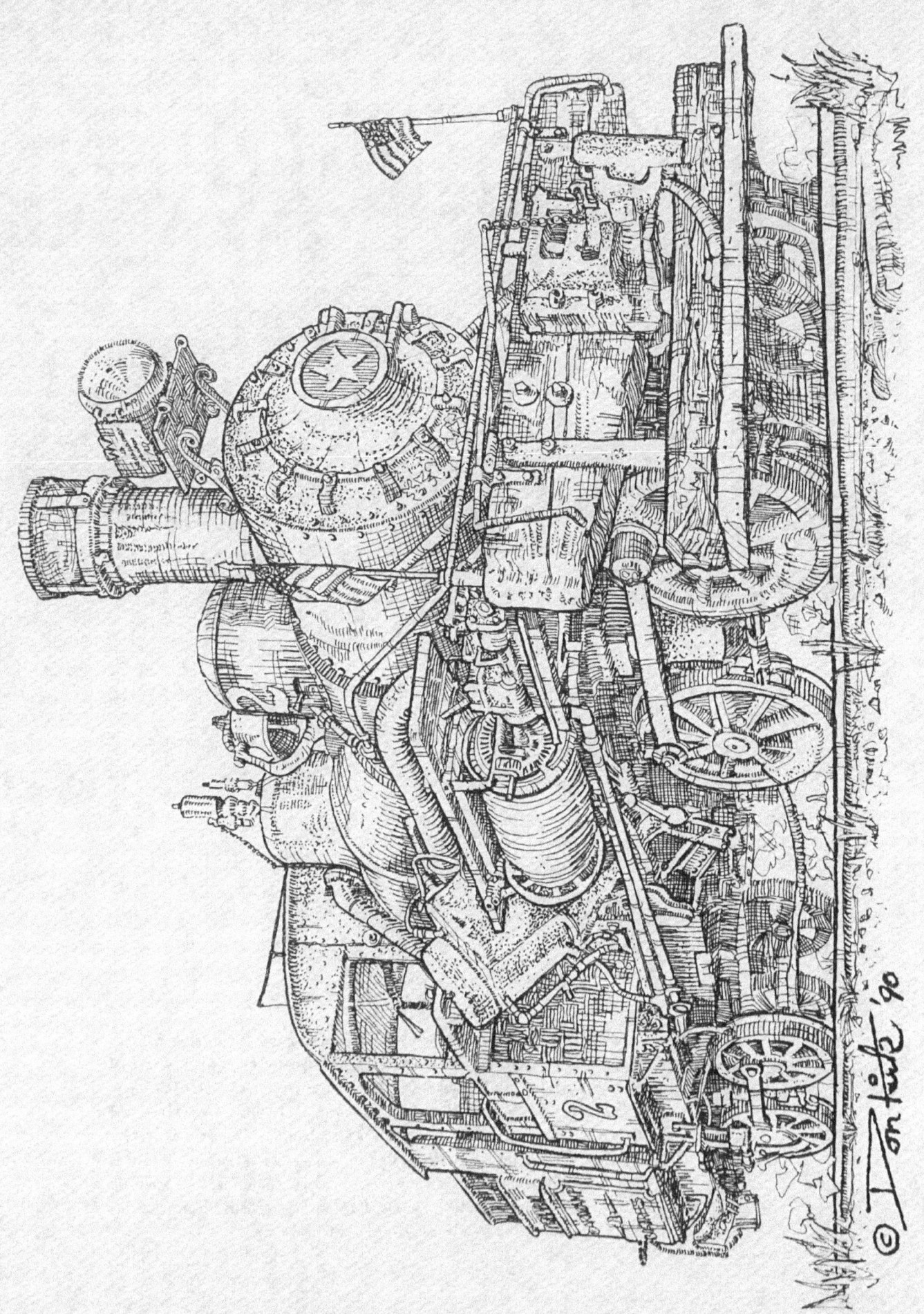

This 1924 Coal Tipple And Sand House On The Cumbres & Toltec Scenic Railroad At Chama, New Mexico Is Known As A 75-Ton Balanced-Bucket Mechanical Coal Tower And Is The Last Remaining Of Three Similar Structures Built For The Denver And Rio Grande Western Railroad. Coal Is Dumped Into A Bin At Ground Level And Then Hoisted By Buckets To The Top Of The Structure. Coal Then Falls By Gravity Down A Chute To The Tender Sitting On The Opposite Side Of The Building. Sand Is Heated And Dried In The Sand House Before It Is Loaded Into The "Sand Dome" On The Top Of The Engine. In Wet Weather On Steep Grades, Sand Is Spread On The Rails In Front Of The Wheels To Prevent Them From Slipping.

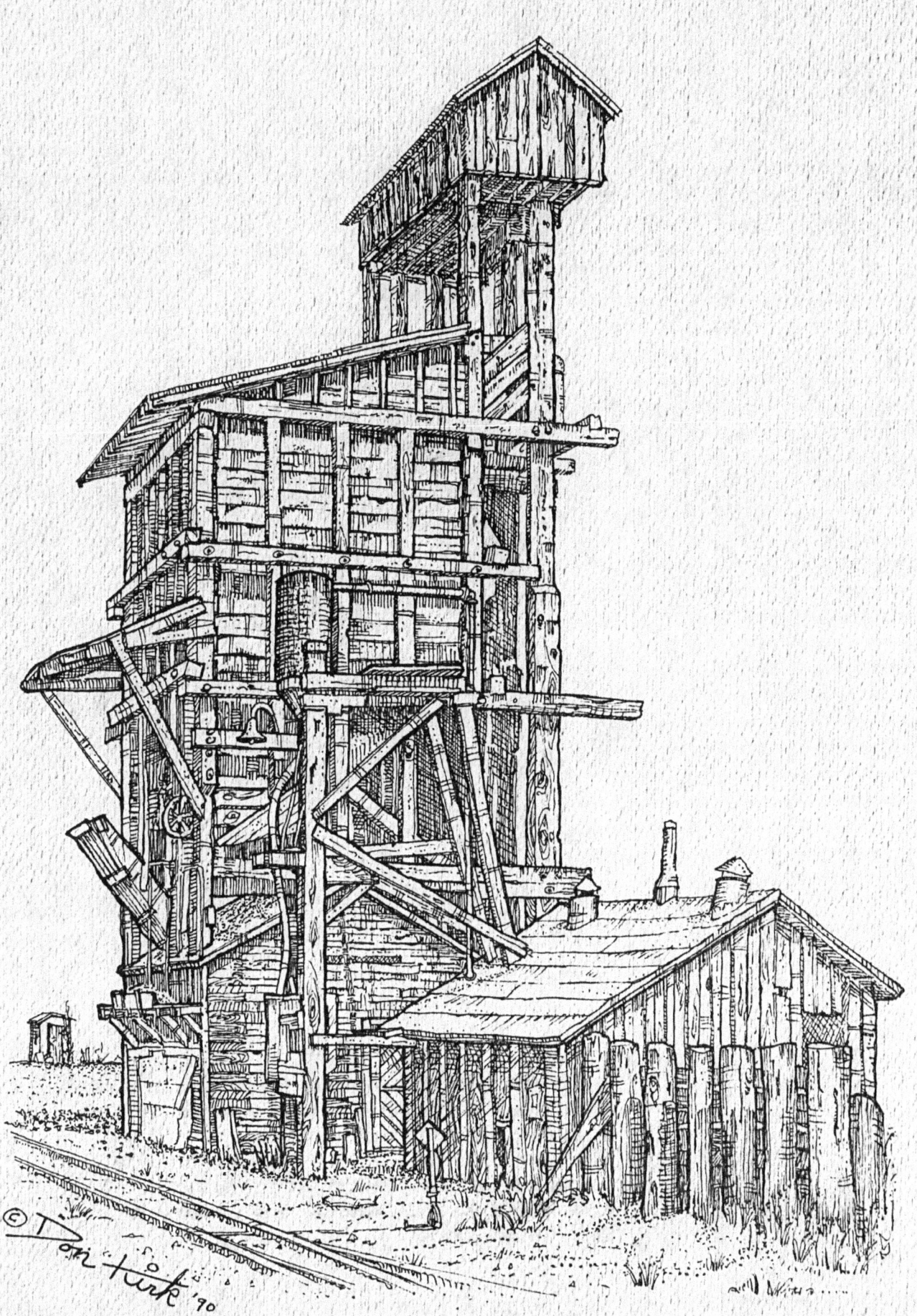

No. "583" Pauses At An 1880'S Style Masonry Railroad Depot At The Colorado
Railroad Museum In Golden, Colorado. The Locomotive Is A Class C-28, 2-8-0
Baldwin Built In 1890 For The Denver And Rio Grande. Over One-Hundred Of
These Locomotives Were Built In 1888 Thru 1892 For Freight Service On The
New Standard Gauge Denver-Pueblo-Ogden Line. With A Weight Of 113,200
Pounds, 46-Inch Drivers, 20X24 Cylinders, And A Boiler Pressure Of 140 Lbs.,
The "583" Produces A Traction Effort Of 24,900 Pounds.

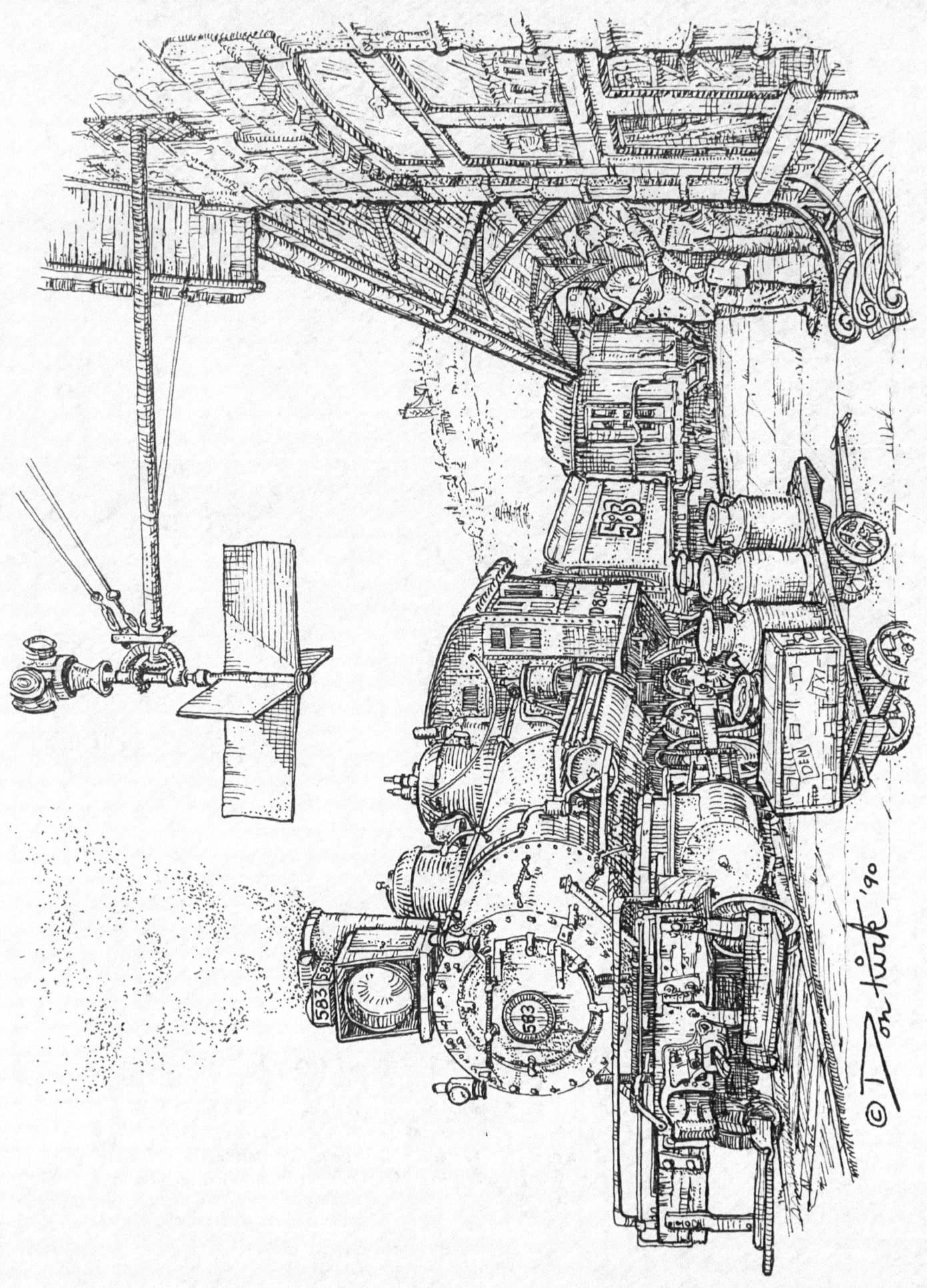

This 77-Ton, Standard Gauge, 1912 Baldwin 0-6-0 Switcher Is An Oil Burner With
A Dummied Up "Coal" Tender Converted By Hollywood For The 1957 Movie "Wings
Of Eagles" Starring John Wayne, Henry Fonda, And William Holden. It Was Built
For The St. Louis & San Francisco Railroad Co. And Has 20-1/2 X 26-Inch Cylinders,
A Boiler Pressure Of 185 Pounds, 51-Inch Drivers, And A Traction Effort Of 33,700
Lbs. It's Now On Display In Front Of The Church Street Station In Orlando, Florida.

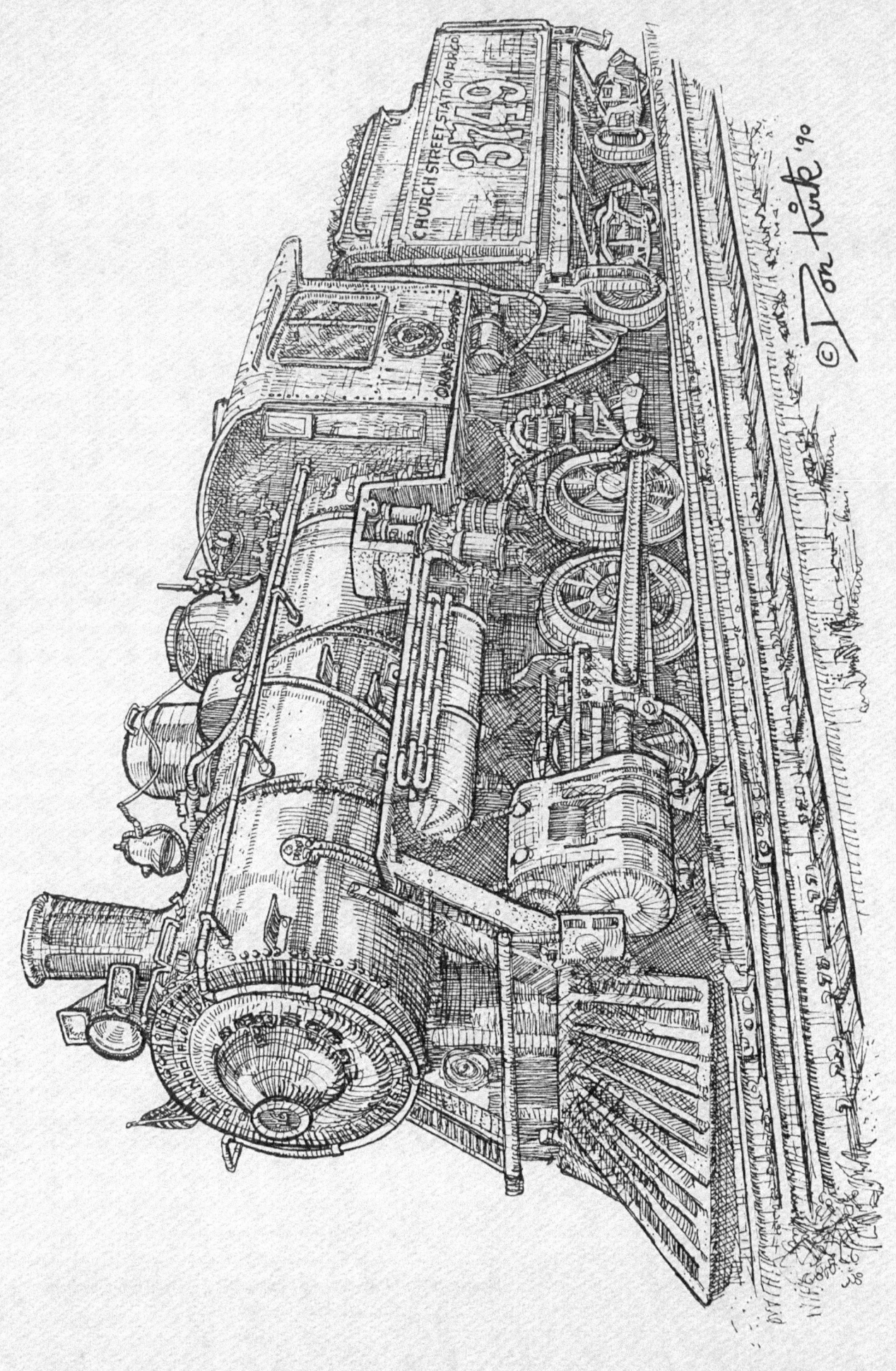

Closeup Of The 77-Ton, Standard Gauge, 1912 Baldwin 0-6-0 Switcher.

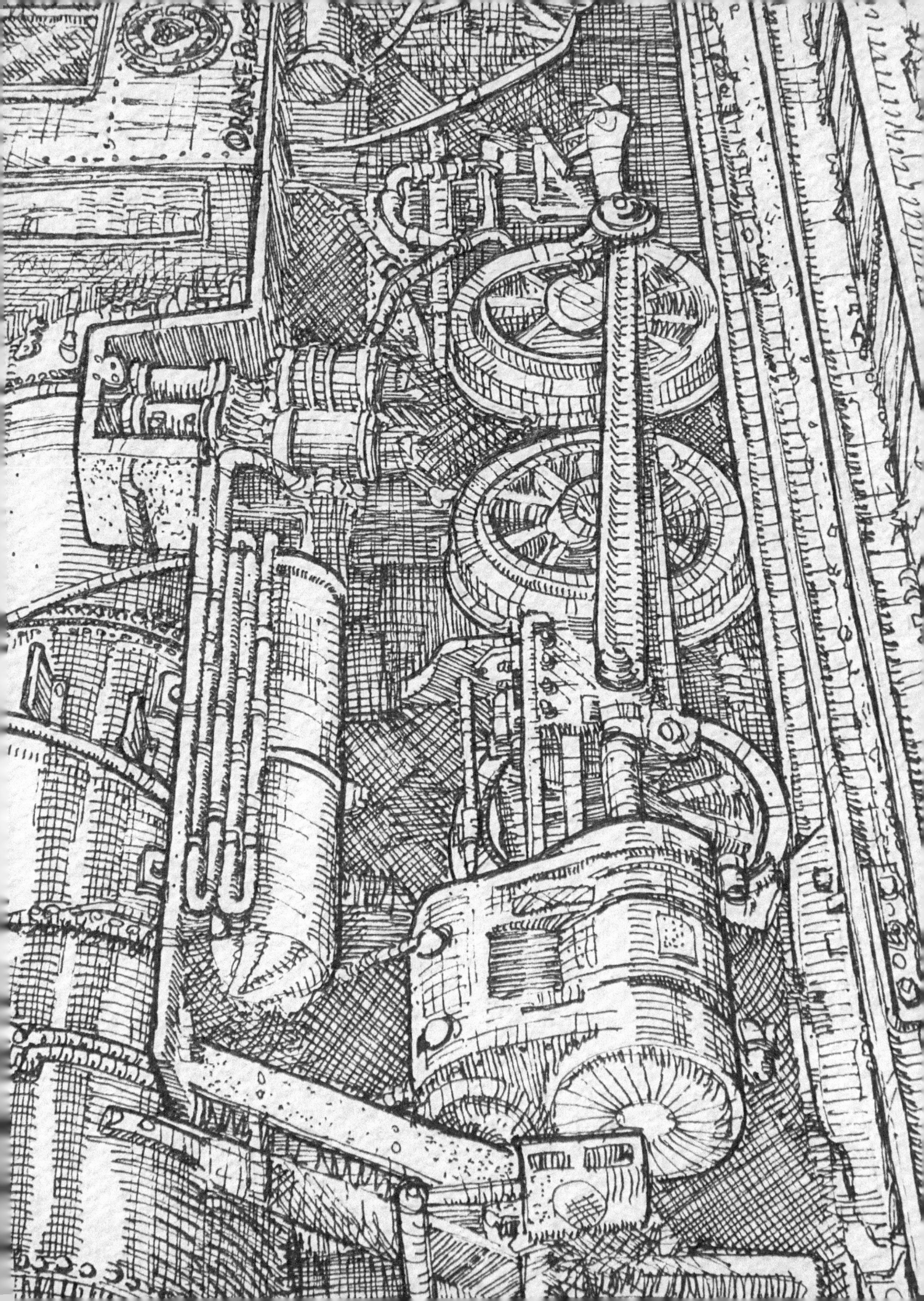

Built In 1910 By The Davenport Locomotive Works, This Narrow-Gauge, Coal-Fired, 2-6-0 "Teakettle" Runs On 31-Inch Drivers, 10 X 16-Inch Cylinders, A Boiler, Pressure Of 150 Pounds And Producers A Traction Effort Of 6,550. This Steam Engine Weights Just 30,000 Lbs. She Is Currently Running At Cedar Point Amusement Park In Sandusky, Ohio.

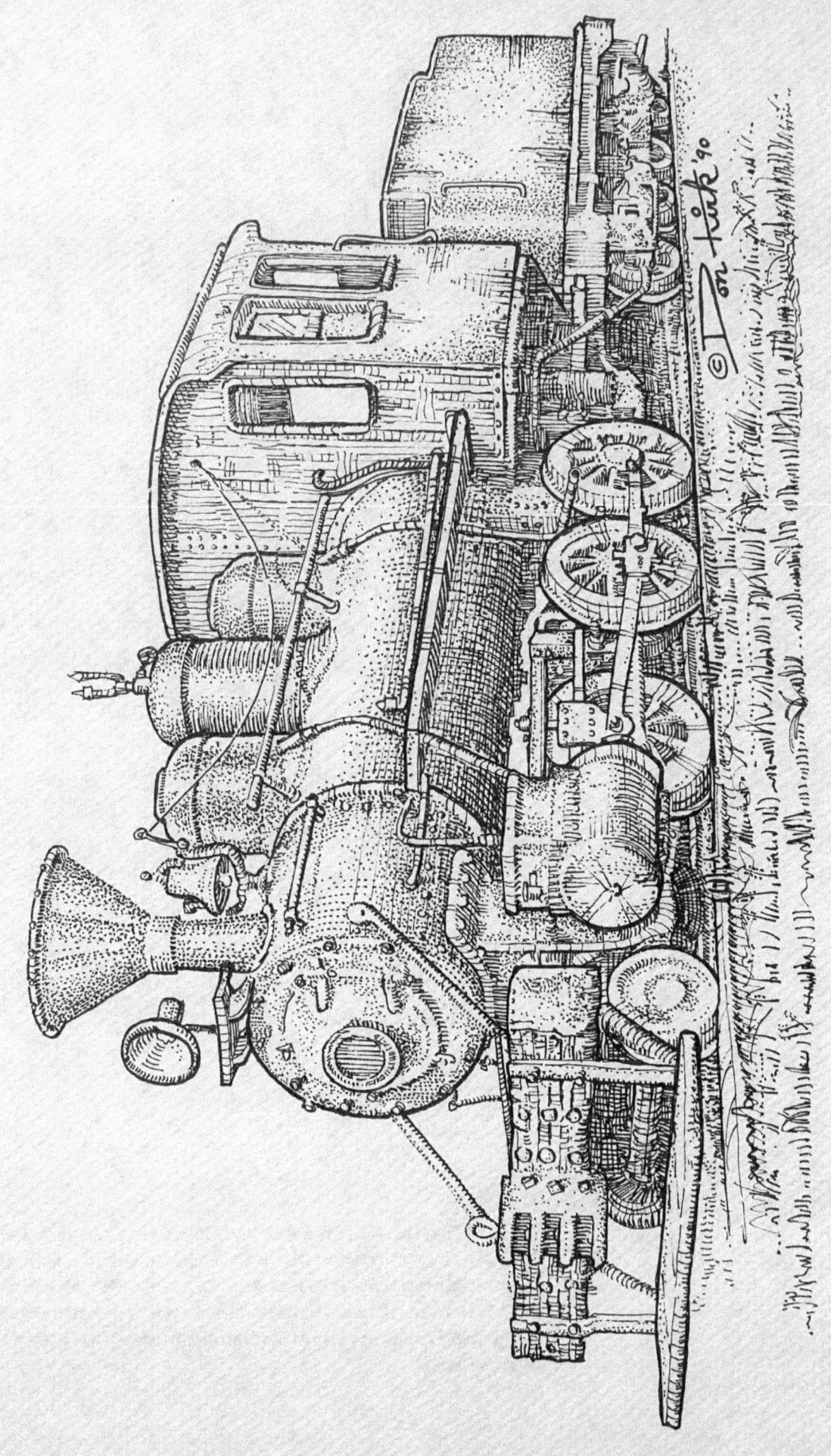

This 1923 Shay Locomotive Is A Coal-Fired, 42-Ton, Geared Steam Engine Built By The Lima Locomotive Works For The Frost-Johnson Lumber Co. At Mansfield, Louisiana. Weighing In At 138,600 Lbs. With 12 X 12 Cylinders, 38-Inch Drivers, And A Boiler Pressure Of 200, This "Old Girl" Produces A Traction Effort Of 23,890 Lbs. Number "3241" Can Be Seen At The Center For Transportation & Commerce In Galveston, Texas.

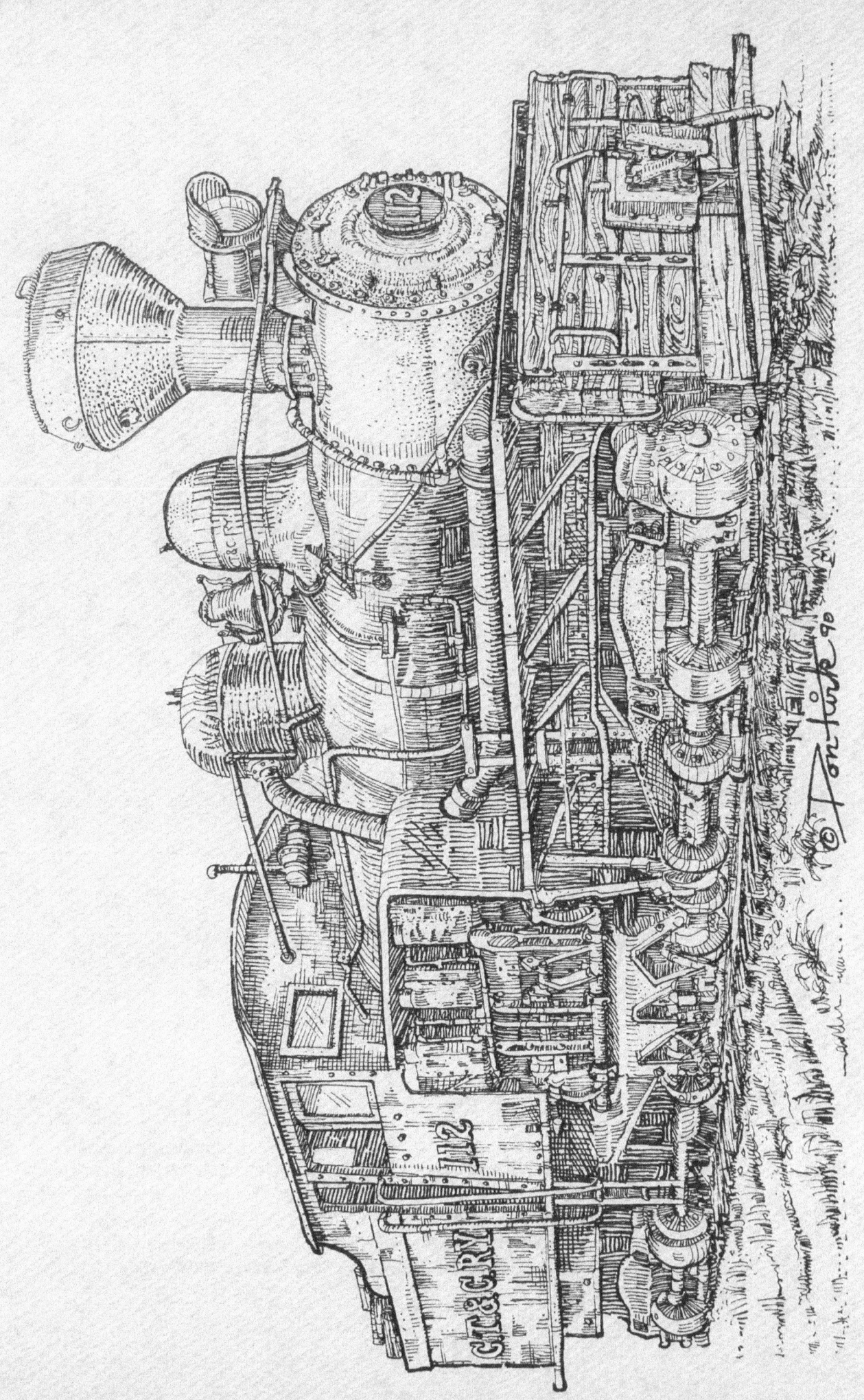

Used In Jungles Hauling Jute, Sugar, Hemp, And Fearful Passengers Who Called It "Toro De Fuego," The Fire Bull. She Was Purchased From The United Railway Of Yucatan, Disassembled For Shipment To The U.S., And Meticulously Renovated Bolt By Bolt So It Could Run On The Walt Disney World Railroad That Encircles The Magic Kingdom. She Is Now An Oil Burner Weighing In At 51,000 Lbs. And Has A Traction Effort Rated At 9,000 Lbs. Her Boiler Pressure Is 150 Pounds.

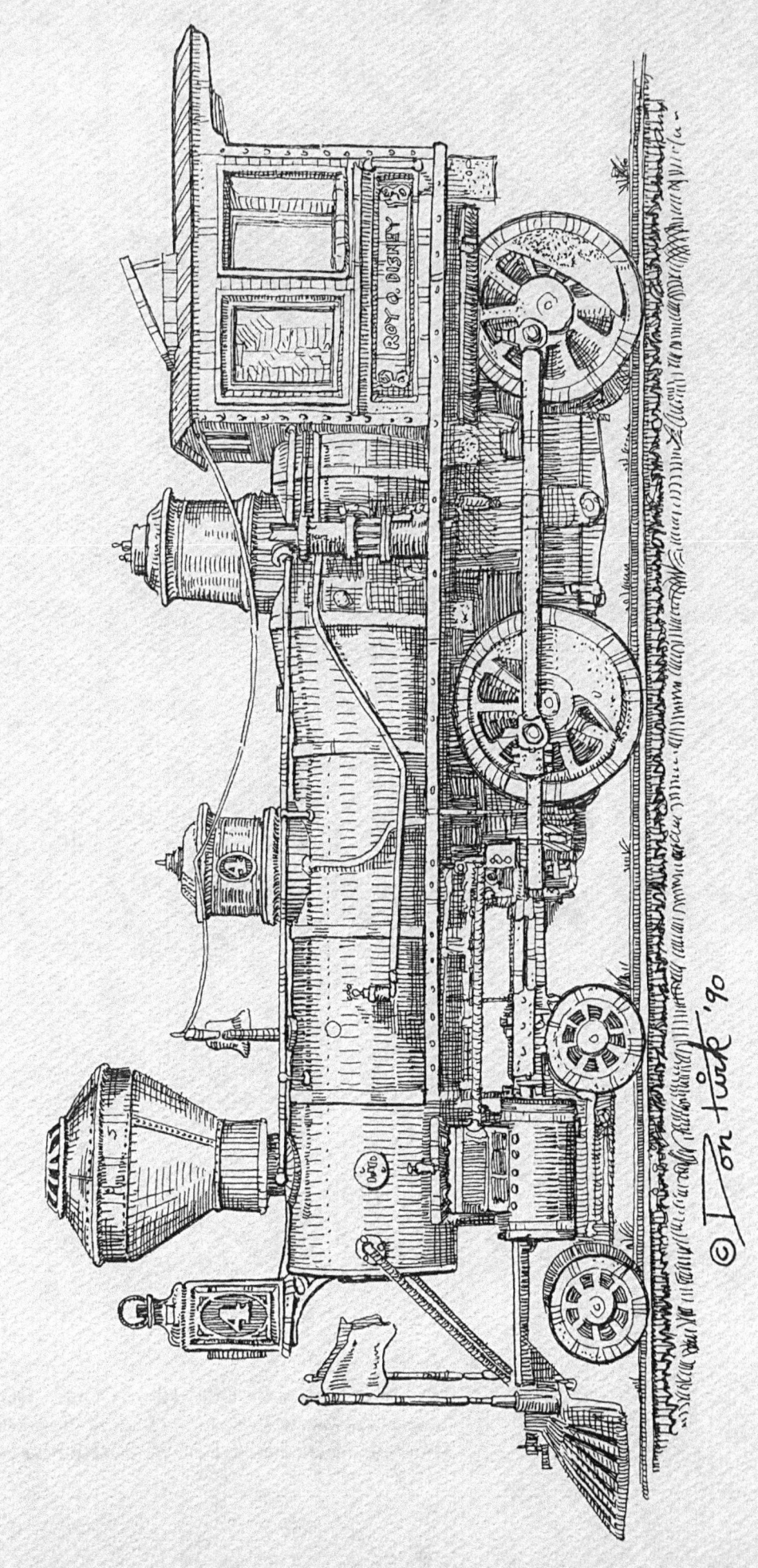

Signal Tower At Ladysmith, British Columbia, Canada. Built In 1898 For The Esquimalt And Nanaimo Railway When A Second Mining Rail Line Crossed Here At An Angle. The Crisscrossing Trains Would Be Controlled By The Signal Tower.

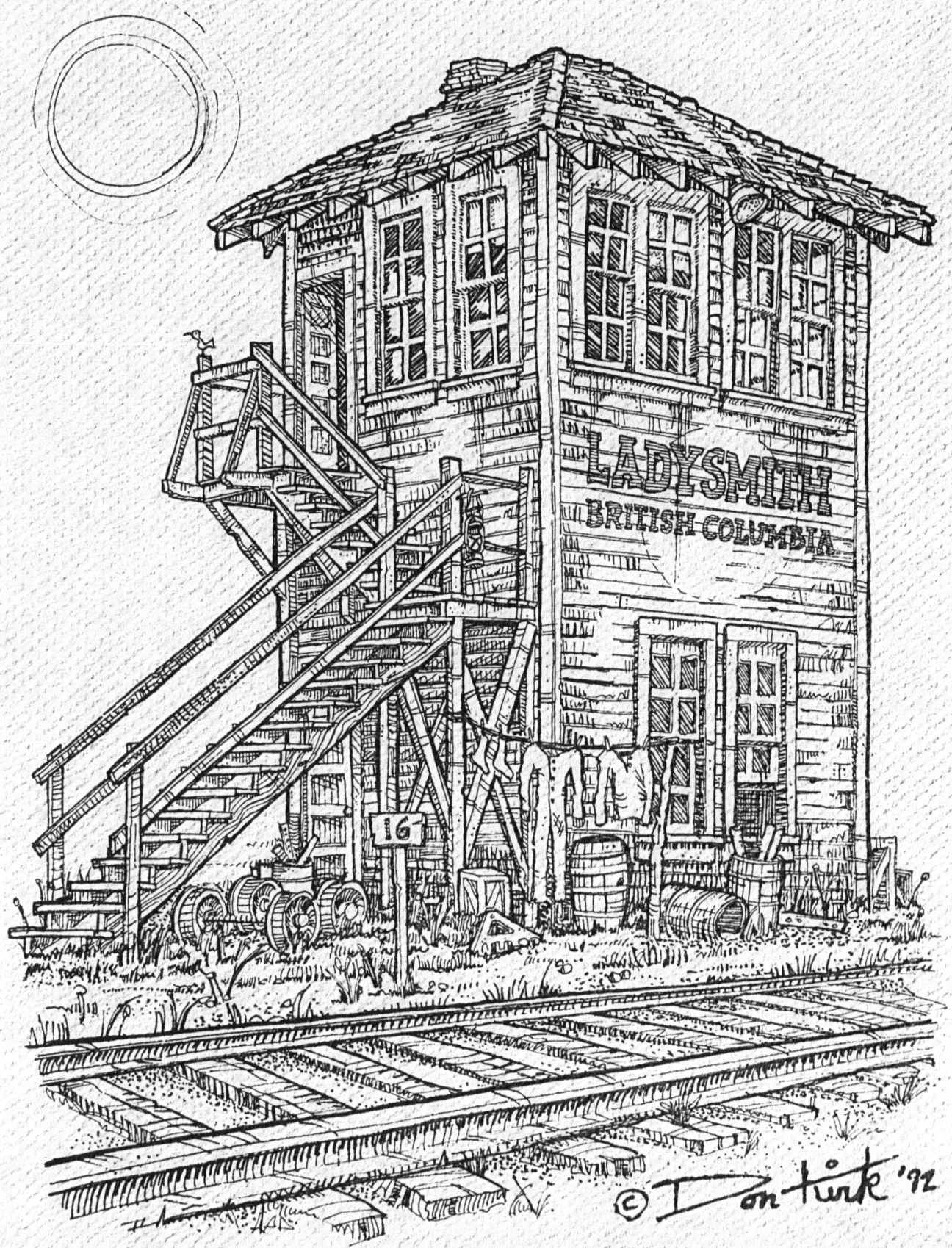

LADYSMITH
BRITISH COLUMBIA

© Don Kirk '92

Sitting On A Spur At The Texas Transportation Museum In San Antonio, Texas
Is A 1911 Baldwin 2-8-0, Oil Burning, Steam Locomotive. Built For W.T. Carter &
Brother Of Camden, Texas, And Given The Number "6." She Last Ran In 1959 On
The Moscow, Camden & San Augestin As A Switcher. She Weights In At 46 Tons,
Has 44-Inch Pistons, A Working Pressure Of 170 Pounds, And A Traction Effort
Rated At 20,000 Pounds.

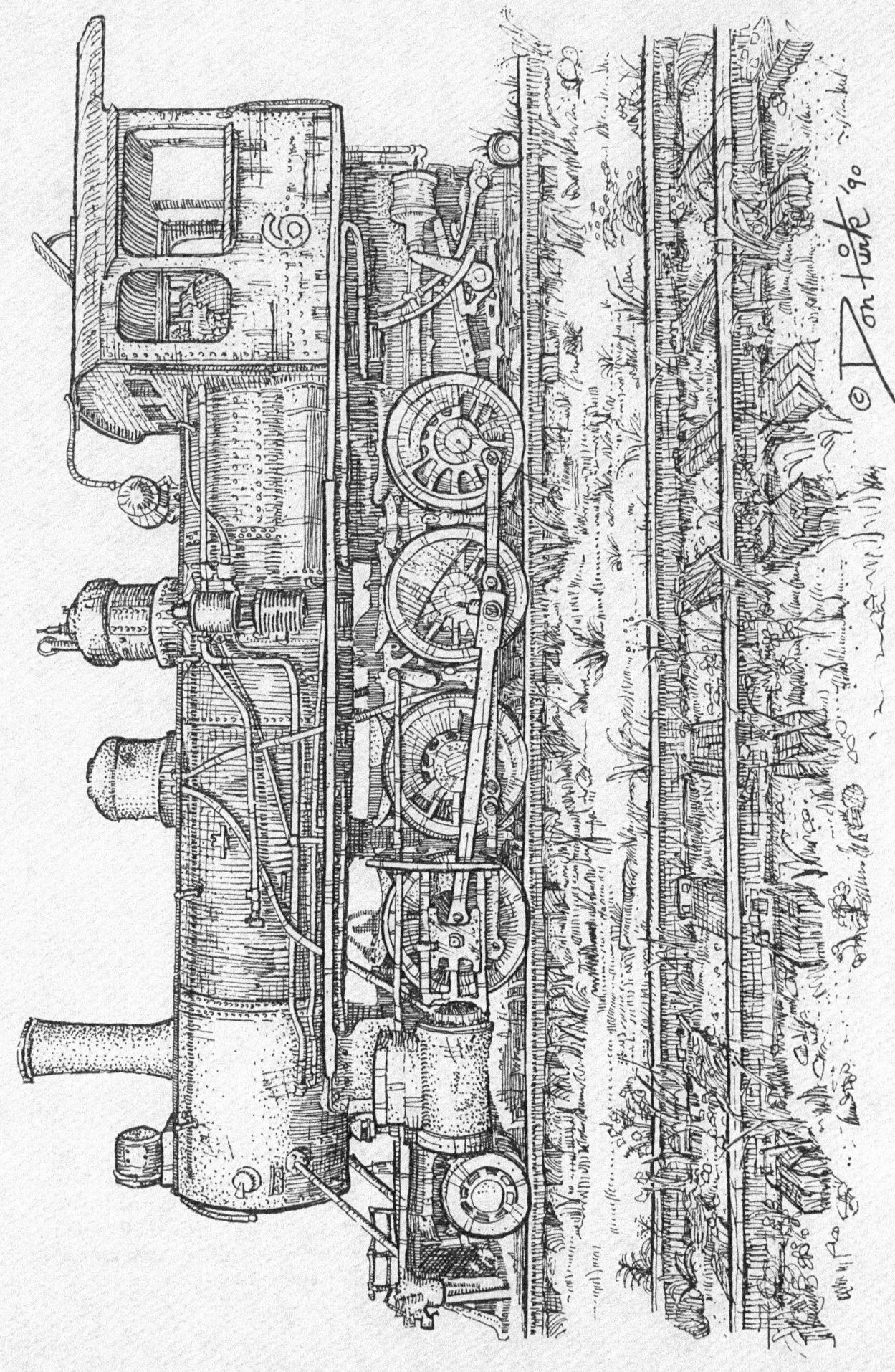

This Rare 2-4-2 Baldwin Steam Engine Built In 1925 For A Hawaiian Sugar Plantation—Hawaii Railway No. 5—Ran Briefly At South Lake Tahoe In 1970 And 1971 On The Tahoe, Trout Creek & Pacific Railroad. This Three-Foot Gauge Engine Had The "Columbia" Wheel Arrangement. It Was Moved To Chama, New Mexico To Run On The Cumbres & Toltic Scenic Railroad But Was Too Light For Travel Over The Cumbres Pass.

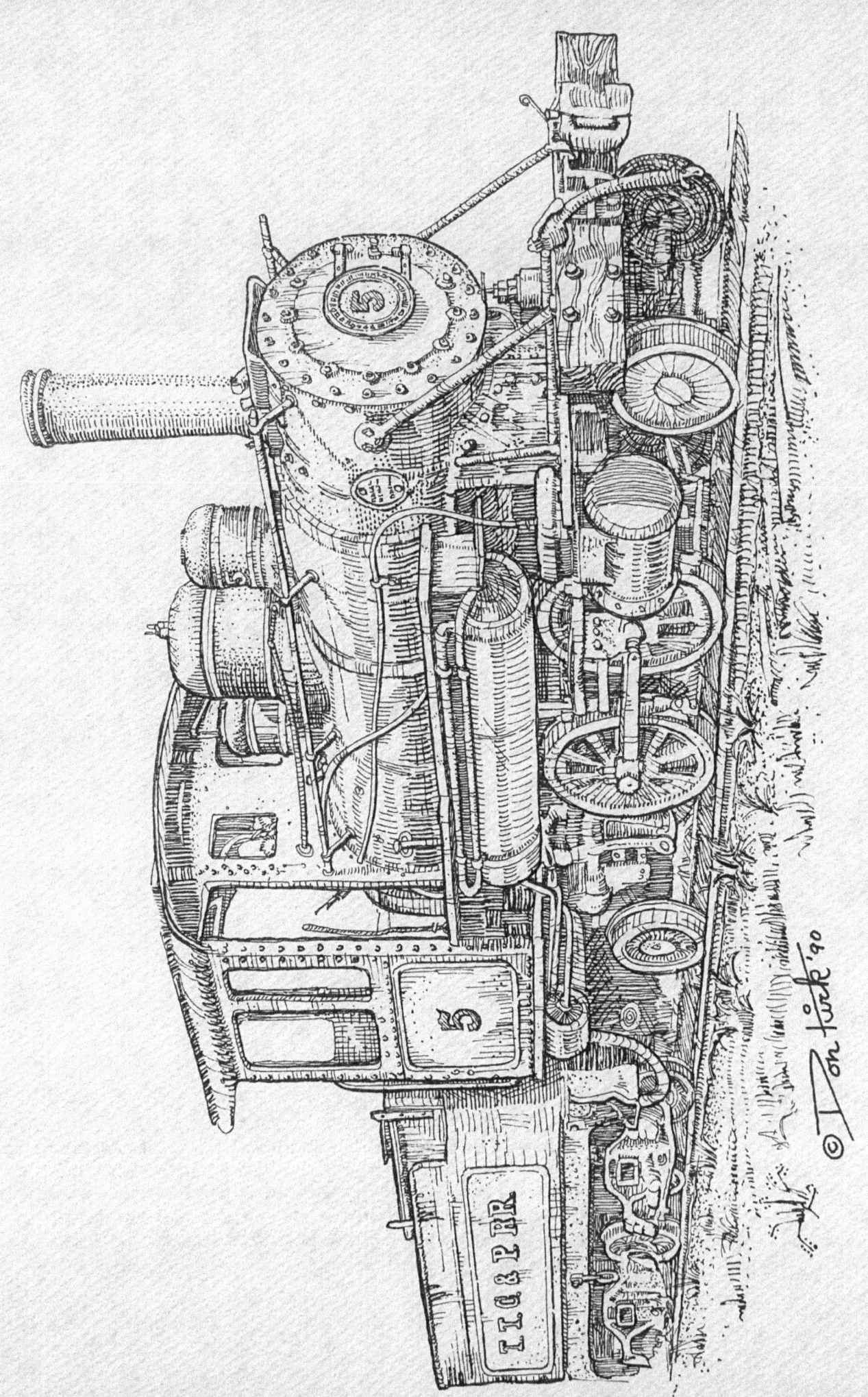

A Side View Of This Rare 2-4-2 Baldwin Steam Engine Built In 1925 For A Hawaiian Sugar Plantation—Hawaii Railway No. 5—Ran Briefly At South Lake Tahoe In 1970 And 1971 On The Tahoe, Trout Creek & Pacific Railroad. This Three-Foot Gauge Engine Had The "Columbia" Wheel Arrangement. It Was Moved To Chama, New Mexico To Run On The Cumbres & Toltic Scenic Railroad But Was Too Light For Travel Over The Cumbres Pass.

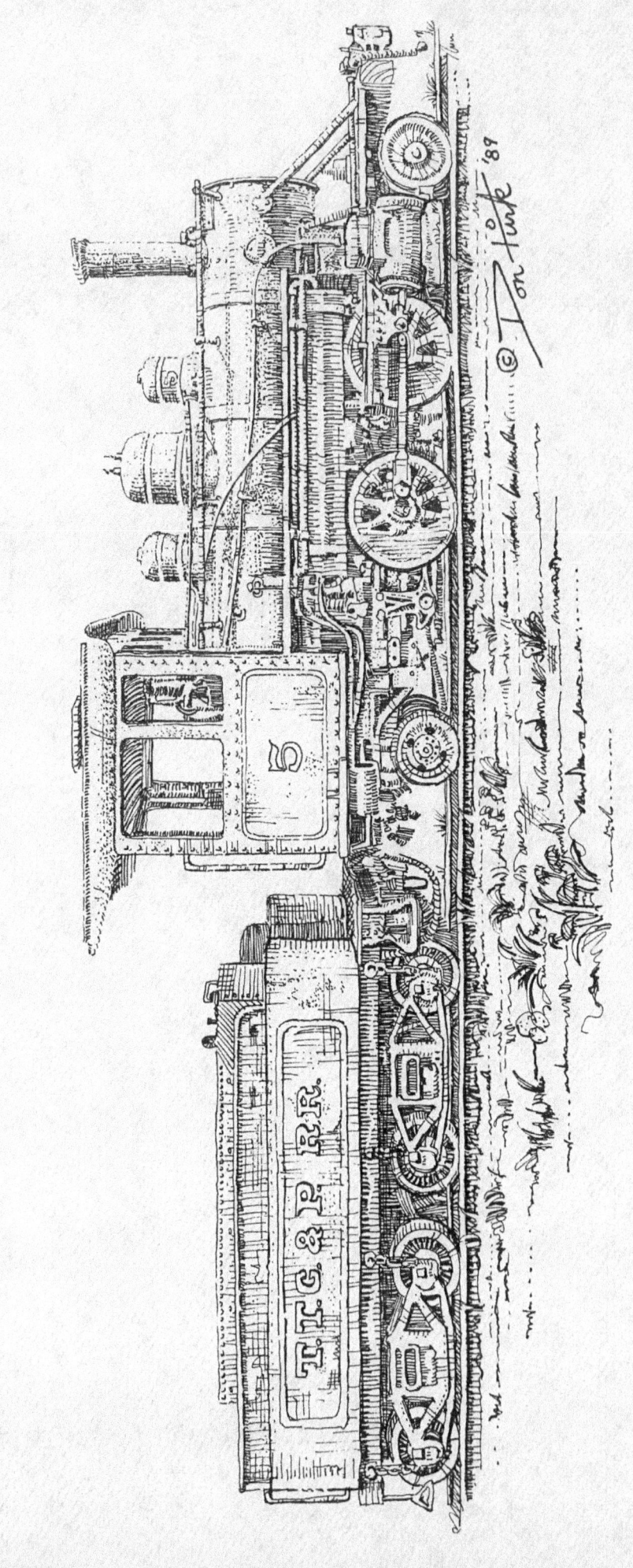

A Montage Of Railroadiana Drawn For Use At The Bottom Of Stationary.

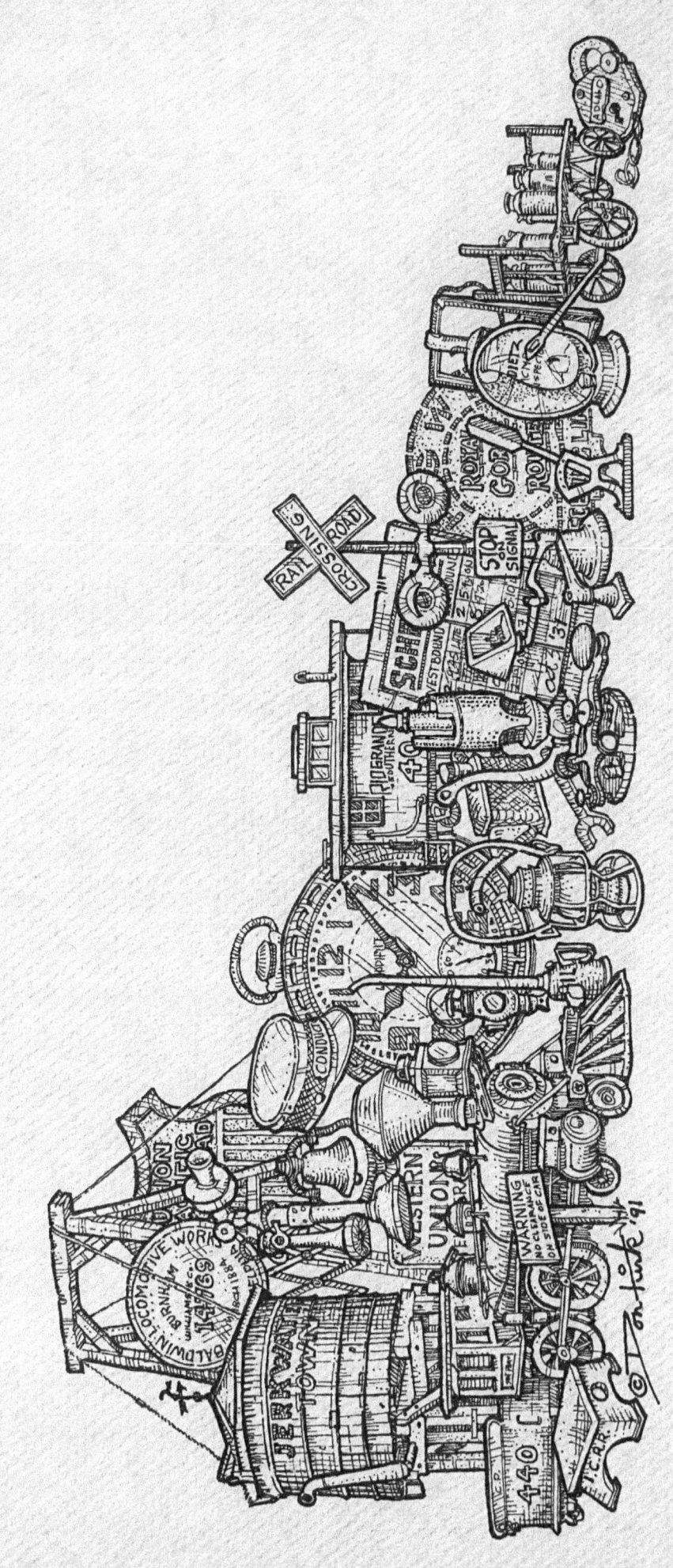

Detail Of The Stationary Artwork.

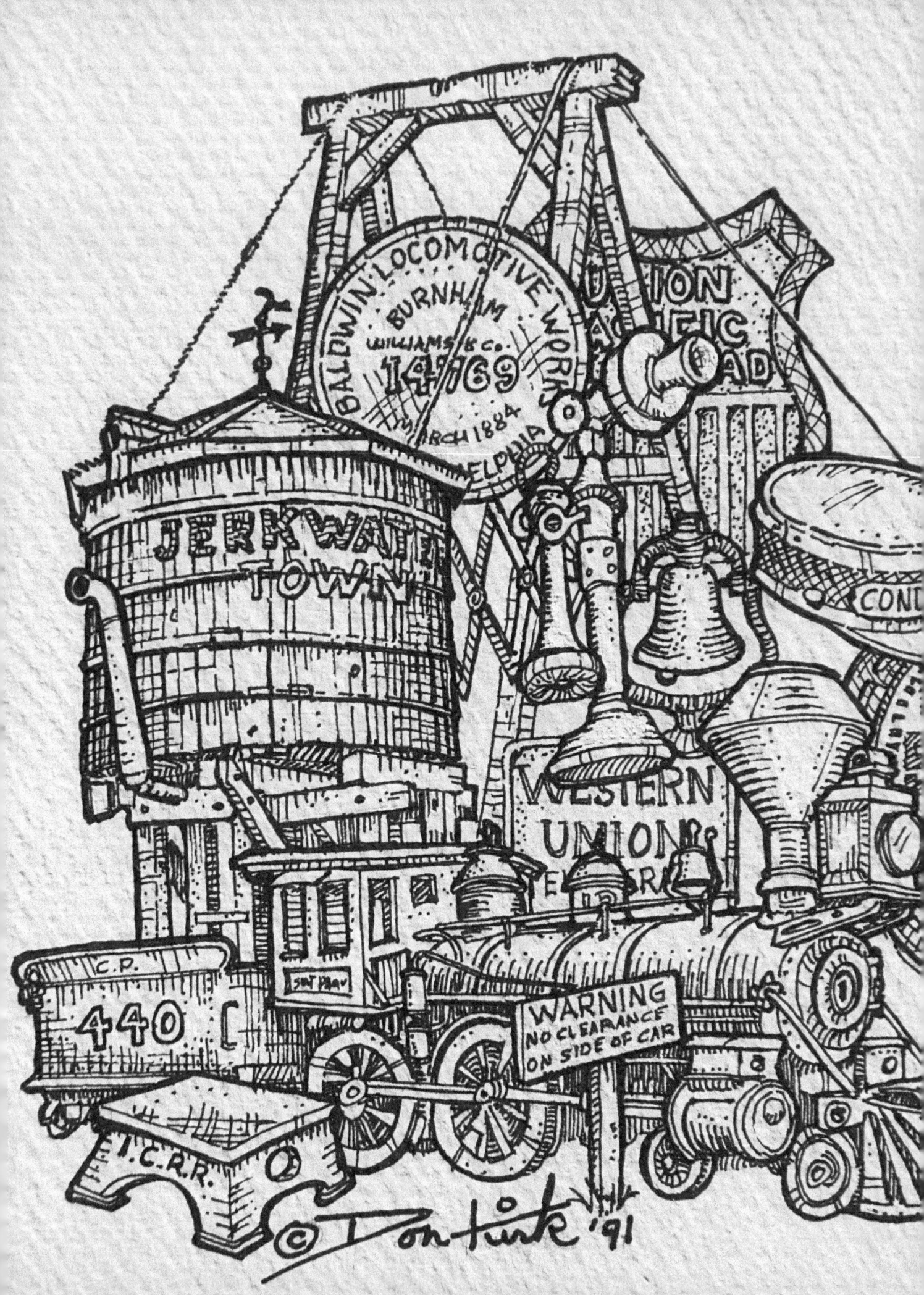

Large Brick Engine House And Smaller Machine Shop Where Steam Engines Are Maintained. The Machine Shop Fabricates And Repairs Steam Engine Parts For The (Fictional) San Antonio & Aransas Pass Railway.

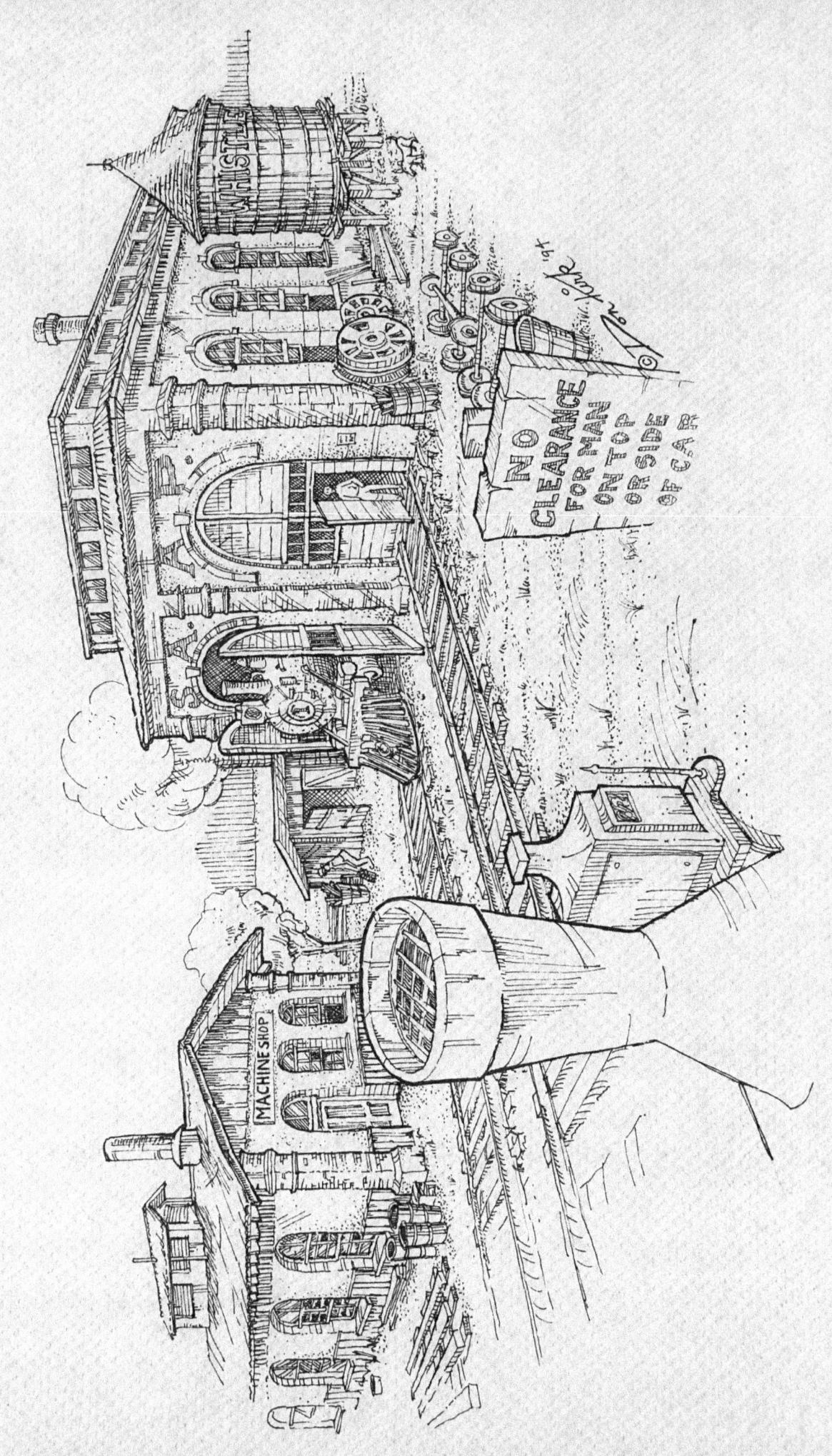

Detail of The Large Brick Engine House And Smaller Machine Shop
Where Steam Engines Are Maintained.

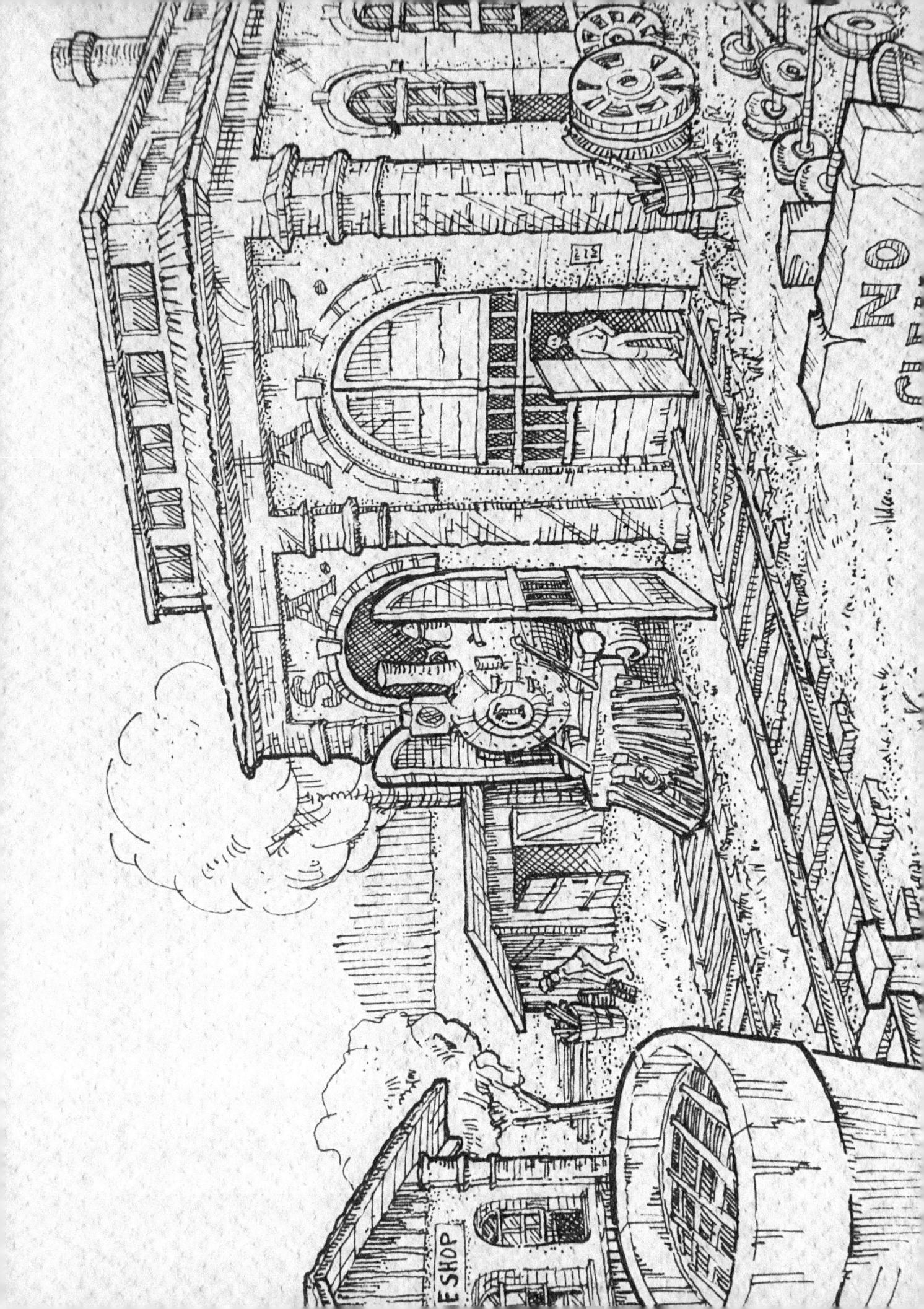

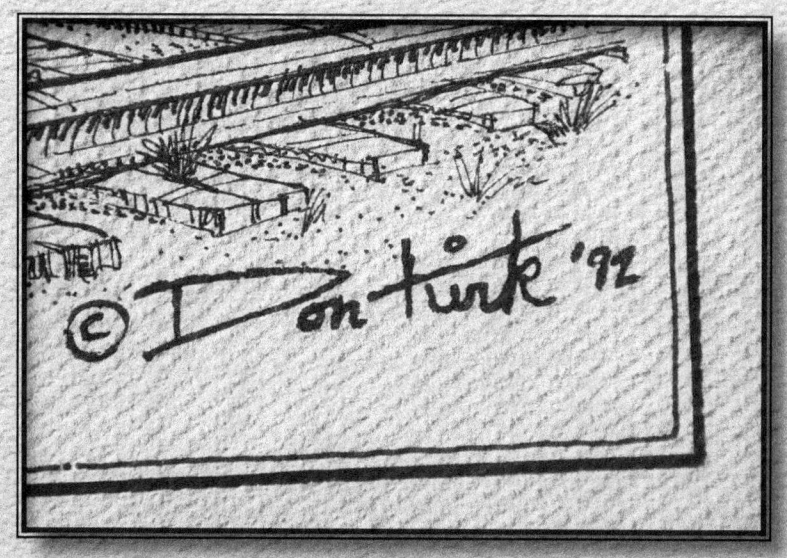

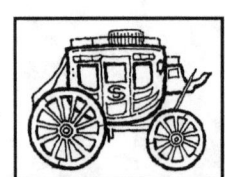

ISBN 978-0-9898004-4-0

www.ingramcontent.com/pod-product-compliance
Lightning Source LLC
Chambersburg PA
CBHW080951170526
45158CB00008B/2441